"*Beside the Empty Cradle* is a wonderful resource for childless couples. The practical information delivered from the heart of someone who knows the pain of infertility and the triumph of God's love for us is invaluable."

—Amber Weigand-Buckley
Editor, OnCourse Magazine

"For years I thought others looked at me as if there was something wrong with me because I didn't have children and didn't adopt. I am so glad that someone is finally addressing the issue that it is okay to follow God's leading in your life and to be okay with being childless."

—Marita Littauer
President, CLASServices, Inc.

BESIDE THE EMPTY CRADLE

FINDING PEACE WITH CHILDLESSNESS

Pamela Sonnenmoser

BEACON HILL PRESS
OF KANSAS CITY

ISBN 978-0-8341-2608-4

Printed in the
United States of America

Cover Design: Darlene Filley
Inside Design: Sharon Page

All Scripture quotations not otherwise designated are from the *New American Standard Bible*® (NASB®), © copyright The Lockman Foundation 1960, 1962, 1963, 1968, 1971, 1972, 1973, 1975, 1977, 1995.

Permission to quote from the following additional copyrighted versions of the Bible is acknowledged with appreciation:

The *Holy Bible, New International Version*® (NIV®). Copyright © 1973, 1978, 1984 by International Bible Society. Used by permission of Zondervan Publishing House. All rights reserved.

The *New King James Version* (NKJV). Copyright © 1979, 1980, 1982 Thomas Nelson, Inc.

The *Holy Bible, New Living Translation* (NLT), copyright © 1996. Used by permission of Tyndale House Publishers, Inc., Wheaton, IL 60189. All rights reserved.

Library of Congress Cataloging-in-Publication Data

Sonnenmoser, Pamela.
  Beside the empty cradle : finding peace with childlessness / Pamela Sonnenmoser.
    p. cm.
  Includes bibliographical references (p.   ).
  ISBN 978-0-8341-2608-4 (pbk.)
  1. Christian women—Religious life. 2. Childlessness—Religious aspects—Christianity. I. Title.
  BV4527.S646 2011
  248.8'43—dc22

2011007388

10 9 8 7 6 5 4 3 2 1

CONTENTS

1
THEN COMES THE BABY IN THE BABY CARRIAGE

Behold, children are a gift of the Lord; The fruit of the womb is a reward.

—Psalm 127:3

As they placed Alexis into my arms, my heart filled with love for this tiny miracle. Her perfect blue eyes fluttered as I stroked the waves of dark hair that fell in tiny ringlets around her face. She was beautiful, completely healthy, and filled with the promise of life.

Her tiny fingers gripped mine as her foot kicked free from the swaddling blanket that wrapped her securely. Each diminutive toe was perfect. I was completely in awe of this beautiful gift from God. I wondered what she would be like as she grew into a toddler and eventually into a wonderful young woman. I held her close to my heart as I rocked her into sweet newborn sleep.

It was amazing how such a small baby could cause such a marvelous reaction in my heart. My chest felt as if it would explode, like baking soda and vinegar in a science fair project. I could feel the tears being forced like a geyser to my eyes. I quickly kissed her forehead and handed the sleeping newborn back to her mother. I could hardly say good-bye as I closed the door to the hospital room. By the time the door had clicked shut behind me, tears were leaping from my eyes. I rushed to my car, escaping into the fortress it provided, and let my tears flow.

I was on an emotional roller coaster. It was exhausting, and I didn't know how much longer I could stand the highs and lows. It had been this way since my husband, John, and I started trying to conceive a child. My mind was consumed with counting days and calculating hours, taking temperatures, allowing excitement to well up each time I thought, *This is the month*. Every time the results came in, "not pregnant," the disappointment hurt more deeply. My heart had calloused over the wounds to the point I could hardly bring myself to express happiness for my friend. My emotions were sandpaper on my soul where my deepest joy and my greatest pain had become conjoined twins.

The child we would have someday consumed every day of our lives. Each passing month pushed "someday" farther away. It was difficult to accept the fact that infertility was becoming an intimate part of our marriage. Three years after we began trying to start our family, it was time to look for answers.

After a physical examination and a few routine tests, my doctor didn't see any reason that I should not be able to get pregnant. At his recommendation, we decided it was time to see a specialist. There were several listed on our insurance. My doctor helped us choose one with a good record of successful pregnancies. The office was an hour from our home, but we would have driven even farther for the chance to become pregnant.

The specialist took tubes of blood and ran a few tests. He said that my hormones were slightly off and put me on Provera, a mild progesterone replacement. After three months, he recommended the use of Clomid, a fertility drug that assists with regular ovulation. He said it would help my body become more fertile. I began taking the drug faithfully and visiting his office every week for a urine test to check hormone levels. If the Clomid worked, we would know right away.

Another three months passed. We were considering which options to try next when we got the call. The most recent test had come back positive—I was pregnant! I could hardly believe it. What perfect timing! It was Father's Day weekend.

I left work early and went straight to find John's very first Father's Day card. I was thrilled to have such a poignant weekend to tell him about our baby. He was as excited as I was. We spent the weekend looking at cribs and bottles, diapers and strollers. We talked about names for boys and girls. We discussed the best schools and thought about looking for a bigger house. There was so much to do before our baby joined our household.

The following Tuesday we went to the doctor for a follow-up appointment and physical examination—and he told us that the pregnancy was not viable. "I'm sorry," he said. "The embryo never attached to the uterine wall."

His explanation was cold. His apologies rang empty and insincere. I was numb. The words were coming through a tunnel. Our baby was gone. We would never know this child whom we had so immediately loved. That night John and I cried together over the child who was not to be. At the doctor's recommendation, we decided to wait six months before we tried again.

Six months later, I was in a wheelchair recovering from a broken hip and pelvis. We could suddenly see God's hand in our lives even through that miscarriage, and we had faith that He was at work. God knew that being pregnant with those injuries would have been detrimental to me and to the baby. I rationalized that He must have been showing us that we would have a child later. He was in control.

I worked hard to recover from a series of surgeries to repair my broken bones. It took almost two years to walk on my own. Our final question for my surgeon was about the safety of a natural childbirth. He said my hip should be just fine and there was no reason to wait any longer. That was exactly what we wanted to hear.

We prayed for guidance as we consulted specialists again. We decided to try Clomid again and proceed cautiously if that didn't work. There were so many options available. It was hard to decide which of modern medicine's developments were in line with our faith and which ones crossed spiritual lines. Neither John nor I were very comfortable with the idea or expense of invitro fertilization, but we had not ruled it out. I was in my early thirties. There was still time.

✳ ✳ ✳

John . . .

Growing up in a farming family, one understands that at least one son will take over the farm operation at some point. In our family that was even-

tually going to be me. That meant I needed a son to take it over from me some day. I wasn't sure if I would be a great dad, because my relationship with my own father wasn't the best. It scared me to think that I might be like him. Still, I thought about all the things I would be able to teach my son. I would take him fishing and hunting, teach him about the land and the way things grow and how amazing God is to have created all of this for us to care for. I looked forward to watching him grow up.

Pamela used to ask me what I would do if we had a girl. I always made some smart comment, but I know I would have loved her and would eventually spend too many hours keeping her away from boys like me. That's just what dads do.

I forced myself to remain unaffected by not having children. I told Pamela that it didn't matter. I didn't have to have kids. In fact, I was pretty good at becoming apathetic about the whole thing. I didn't think about the fact that my apathy left her feeling alone as she dealt with changing hormones and the need to become a mother.

My neutral position changed the day she told me she was pregnant. Suddenly it wasn't an abstract idea for some other day. It was real—I was going to be a father. I was going to raise a child who would become my legacy. Apathy could not remain where so much love immediately arrived.

For a few days, I loved in a way I never knew I could. Then, as fast as it had come, it was gone. I had never felt such a gut-wrenching pain. Pamela started talking about trying again later. I could not see why she would want to go through this again. It hurt too much.

Apathy makes a good anesthetic. It may not heal the wound, but at least I didn't have to feel it. I had to shut down my emotions so that I wouldn't think about the son who might have been. I couldn't watch her cry anymore. This was not the way it was supposed to be.

When Pamela's hip broke, it was almost a relief that she wasn't pregnant. I don't know how we could have chosen what to do for her if we had our unborn child to consider. During her recovery from multiple surgeries, there was a reprieve for me. For the first time in years, we weren't worried about getting pregnant.

It was nice to enjoy just being together without so much pressure. Even with the wheelchair, crutches, and hospital stays, I felt closer to Pamela than I had in a long time. I thought maybe she would get pregnant more easily when we were ready to try again.

* * *

Pamela . . .

As little girls we dream of the day we will meet the man God created for us: Prince Charming. I had planned my wedding and my family by the time I was in fifth grade. I would get married at twenty-five and have my first baby, a boy, before I turned twenty-seven. Being a mother was part of the package.

Do you remember playing house? Every generation of little girls has argued over who gets to play the role of the mom. The boys take turns being the dad. Even when we were preschoolers, something told us that parenting was the best part to play.

By sixth grade, teasing one another over who likes whom has become a favorite pastime. "Jimmy and Suzie sittin' in a tree, K-I-S-S-I-N-G. First comes love, then comes marriage, then comes the baby in the baby carriage."

I knew in high school what I would name my first child. It would be a girl, and her name was Aubrilyn Paige. Most of my friends had chosen names too. In high school, we were assigned an egg or sack of flour to carry around for a week. The care of our pretend children was graded very seriously. They had to be fed, clothed, and cared for twenty-four hours a day.

Schools across the nation have invested in these types of classes to teach young people the proper care of babies. Most of us named our pretend infants according to our plan for a real future baby. We cared for the tiny project and even argued with our appointed parental counterpart over the care of the pseudo-child.

When we grow up and become serious about a relationship, one of the first things we discuss is the number of children we want. We dream about sons and daughters who will come to bless our family someday.

My friend Tamara Clymer, a writer and speaker, started planning her future with her husband and children while still in high school. Tamara shares her story:

The time I first saw Shad and watched him play a pickup basketball game from across the gym, I knew in the way only a seventh-grader can that I had found my soul mate. As is typical with adolescent boys, it took a while for him to figure it out. By my eighth-grade graduation, we were an item, and we never looked back.

Over the next five years we chatted in the hall by our lockers, rode the bus to ballgames, and attended homecomings and proms. We planned our futures and dreamed of the family we would some-day have. He wanted two kids; I dreamed of four. He wanted girls, and I preferred boys. We finally settled on three in whatever com-bination God decided would be best. We were absolutely sure we could plan our family the way we would plan a summer vacation.

Our life was unfolding on schedule. We were married on a warm September day in my sophomore year of college. I went on the pill to make sure the timing of our plan stayed on track. We planned to start our family in two years when we were ready to graduate. We thought getting pregnant in time for the baby to ar-rive the summer after graduation was the perfect plan.

By our third anniversary we realized our plan was unraveling. It was clear that something was wrong. After twelve months of trying to start our family, we were not pregnant. We hadn't seen as much as one late cycle.

Our family doctor convinced us to calm down and keep trying. "Surely it will happen soon," he assured.

But it didn't. Month after month we expected to be expecting. Our hopes and dreams rose and fell every twenty-eight days.

After several months, we set up another appointment with the doctor. He ordered a battery of tests that ended up being just the beginning of probing, temperature charts, medication, and even more stress. Over the next few years our lives became consumed with trying to have a baby.

Month after month our hopes were raised and dashed. It was the only thing dependable about my monthly cycle: a few days of trying, a week and a half of waiting, then the crash of disappoint-ment—only to start the whole thing over again two weeks later. Every month we were sure: *This will be the month our dreams will come true.* But it wasn't.

We prayed. Actually it was more like begging. We begged God to give us a child. We made deals with Him, pleading for His blessing of children, earnestly hitting our knees before the Father. We spent sleepless nights crying out for His help. But as our fifth, sixth, and seventh anniversaries came and went, we slowly started coming to terms with God's answer to our prayers.

We were childless, and it appeared that drugs, surgery, and medical probing would not change that fact. What we had taken for granted—our perfect plan—was quickly consuming our lives. What had started as our dream had become a nightmare.

Tamara's story of shattered dreams and dashed hope resonates with millions of childless families around the world. We never dream of the day when we will sit in a sterile exam room and hear the words "You will not be able to have children." The emotions that those words evoke are indescribable. A combination of anguish, denial, and panic twists through our minds.

In the United States alone there are more than 2.1 million (7.4 percent) married couples who are unable to conceive a child.[1] According to the Centers for Disease Control, 7.3 million women ages 15-44 have impaired fecundity, the impaired ability to have children. That is 11.8 percent of all women in the United States. These numbers are contrary to the feelings of isolation and aloneness that shadow those going through the infertility experience.

Infertility treatments range from herbal potions and home remedies passed through generations to advanced medications that prompt ovulation and stimulate hormones. Scientific advances have come a long way in assisting with conception. Methods such as artificial insemination (AF) and in vitro fertilization (IVF) are widely practiced worldwide.

There is some controversy in the Church about IVF due to the use of cryogenic embryos that were thought of as science fiction only a few years ago. The question of what to do with harvested, fertilized eggs that are cryogenically frozen should be considered before a couple moves forward with this type of infertility treatment. There are options, such as donating them to a fertilization clinic or embryonic bank, where they are cryogenically contained until a matching mother seeks to adopt them.

There is never a shortage of people who are willing to share the best methods with the childless couple. When John and I had been unable to conceive a child for more than a year, a friend called with the answer. Her grandmother's cousin had used this remedy, and it worked so well that she had seven children. All I had to do was to cut strips of virgin flannel and soak them in lanolin. I was instructed to lay them in a woven pattern over my abdomen for one hour each night. Fresh flannel would be required each time. In truth, some studies link lanolin to infertility, and many people are allergic to it.[2]

In this epidemic of infertility, many couples try various remedies and cures and then find themselves the proud parents of multiple children. Others decide to forgo medical treatments and pursue adoption to fill their nests and their hearts. There are thousands of stories of miracle children—wonderful gifts from God after infertility.

My friend Siobhan's story is like that of many other infertile couples. According to doctors, she and her husband should have never conceived a child. In their desire to fill their home with more children, the couple discovered what a gift their only child is. They also gained insight and compassion for those who are permanently childless.

"I am one of those people who have been irregular all of their lives," Siobhan told me. "I have known since I got married that having children was going to be close to impossible."

Siobhan's diagnosis was polycystic ovarian syndrome, the most common cause of female infertility. "I had almost all of the symptoms," she said.

Siobhan and her husband tried Clomid, temperature-taking, and everything else her doctor suggested to try to get pregnant.

"Nothing worked. We more or less gave up and just went back to life as normal."

In the middle of the summer of 2001 Siobhan noticed soreness in her breasts. Coworkers tried to convince her that she was pregnant.

"I laughed, because I knew it just wouldn't happen to me like that. I even took a pregnancy test, and it was negative," she said.

Her symptoms were persistent, so a week later she took another test. "I was shocked when it was positive," she said, unable to contain her joy even seven years later.

Garrett was born twelve weeks early and weighed only 2.76 pounds. "We were scared, but we knew God had given us this little guy. We prayed that He would allow him to stay with us. Today Garret is a perfectly healthy little boy.

Siobhan got pregnant again in 2002 but miscarried. They were devastated. In 2004 they decided to try again with the help of a fertility specialist.

"We were told that Garrett was a fluke," Siobhan said. "The doctors said I shouldn't have gotten pregnant with him. I knew that whether a fluke or not, he was a gift from God. I was obviously supposed to have gotten pregnant with him."

"However," she continued, "after giving myself shots in the stomach, taking pills, two IUI's [intrauterine insemination], and spending more money than we could afford, we knew it was time to give up trying to conceive again."

Siobhan has never been able to have a second child. "I know it doesn't compare with a lot of people's stories, but infertility touches people in so many ways. The realization that your own body has failed you is a shock."

Stories like Siobhan's give many childless couples hope that one day they will have the thing they want the most: a child to love, a child to raise to be a wonderful adult, a child to teach the things of God, a little someone who will know that he or she is the biggest blessing in life. What happens when that hope does not come? What happens when the chance to become a parent is ripped away forever?

Newlyweds don't usually worry if they haven't conceived in the first year or so of marriage. Most doctors won't even consider fertility testing or treatment until a couple has been unsuccessfully trying to become pregnant for six months if they are over thirty-five, or a year for younger couples.[3]

Some couples may even count it a blessing to have time to grow together and fall into their roles as husband and wife before adding the joy of children to the home. By the second or third full year of marriage without a pregnancy, though, most couples have consulted their doctor and tried simple methods like ovulation prediction to try to conceive their first child.

Soon the questions from friends and relatives sneak into casual conversations. Parents on both sides are wondering when their grandchildren will come. As friends begin to start their families, a twinge of panic accompanies each baby shower invitation.

Infertility check:
- Have you been trying to get pregnant for more than two years?
- Have you ever had a miscarriage?
- Have you had issues with obesity or rapid weight gain?
- Do you have irregular or missing menstrual cycles?
- Have you ever been told by a physician that you might have trouble conceiving or carrying a child?

If you answered yes to any of these questions, you should see your gynecologist to determine if you are experiencing issues of infertility. If you answered yes to three or more of these questions, you should consider seeing a fertility specialist.

The summer I turned thirty-one, it seemed as if ninety percent of my friends had newborns or were pregnant. I received a baby shower invitation at least once a week. Cute little cutout booties, baby bottles, and rattles urged us to share the joy of the new arrivals. Every invitation required a trip to stores with names like "Babies-R-Us" and "Children's Orchard." Mulling over the many items listed on gift registries was torture: tiny baby shoes, cuddly baby blankets, the newest technology in baby monitors. By the end of the summer, opening mail became a chore. I sorted envelopes, choosing to open bills before anything that was hand-addressed.

The fun in silly shower games eluded me. I didn't want to guess what was in the bassinette, I didn't care if I got the mustard-filled diaper, and guessing which baby food was being spooned into my mouth did not make me crave baby showers.

Making small talk with women I hardly knew was the hardest part of the shower circuit. Every conversation included a question about children. "Do you have kids?" "How many kids do you have?" Although questions like those are conversation-starters for most people, to the infertile woman they are enough to start a flood of tears.

There is no correct response. If you simply say you have no children, the next question, predictably, begins an interrogation to find the reason.

If you say you don't have any children *yet*, you open the door to twenty minutes of pseudo-encouragement and tales of how they or someone close to them got pregnant. Finally, if the conversation identifies you as infertile, it will invoke an awkward silence followed by stories of miracle pregnancies intended to encourage. The whole thing is exhausting and invasive. It didn't take long until the dread of those conversations kept me from attending baby showers totally.

I eventually enlisted the help of a sympathetic friend to shop for baby gifts for me. I made excuses not to attend the showers and just dropped the gifts off when I knew the mother-to-be wasn't home. It wasn't that I wasn't happy for my friends—I just didn't want to ruin their special days by having to excuse myself early or by walking out in tears. It was better simply to stay home.

The last thing I wanted to talk about was infertility. It was like the elephant in the room—always there for everyone to see.

If you have had an experience like mine, deep down you know at some point the truth will have to be acknowledged. Once we accept our infertility, we can begin to come to terms with it. At that point, accepting that we will not have a biological child leaves us searching for hope. We cling to faith that God will somehow bring a miracle child into our family—and sometimes, through a miracle pregnancy or adoption, He does.

But only sometimes. For many infertile couples the choices run out, and miracles are withheld for reasons they don't understand. Coming to terms with permanent infertility is nearly impossible for some couples, but it is also the first step toward healing. If we keep our focus on the Lord, He will draw us close during the trial of infertility, and our relationship with Him will grow.

North Carolina native Lynn Fries shares her infertility story with other childless women to lend support during their despair.

When we began to plan for our family, it seemed that other couples around us just thought, "Let's have a baby," and it happened. We thought the same thing, but pregnancy eluded us. While our struggle to become parents was a source of great pain, it also fostered in us a complete dependence on the Lord. We knew the closeness we gained in our relationship with Christ would be the core of our family when that gift finally came.

We kept waiting for our miracle, believing it would come. We were childless, but we were happy. We trusted that a baby would join our family when it was God's time for it to happen.

When we found out we were permanently unable to conceive a child, we were forced to deal with our infertility on a different level. We had to be put the dream to rest. People in the church talk about victory over trials and fighting to get the reward when faced with challenges in life, but what do you do when you fight a hard fight and the reward never comes?

We were still waiting on the Lord, knowing we would love any child the Lord chose to give us. It felt as if the whole universe were fighting against our having a child to love. After the hysterectomy, we considered adopting an older child, but we were afraid even to hope that it could happen, and we didn't know if we had the energy, money, or time to go down one more road that could be a dead-end.

We wanted to know all the joys and challenges that come with being a parent. We still do. We have grieved for the children we won't have. Many times we have been spectators in life, watching others live the things we dreamed. The reminders are constant. The grief is greater some days than others. It comes unexpectedly most of the times.

Simply seeing a mom with a baby stroller can bring me to tears. Sometimes it is just a flash of pain, while other times the anguish lingers. It can be like a scratch on the surface or feel as if it's tearing my heart out. The hardest part is not knowing when it will hit. We can anticipate it, try to prepare for it, but it's as if the grief has a life of its own.

We will never have the joy of seeing our children take their first steps, open their Christmas stockings, or go off to school. We won't bake cookies with them, watch them grow up, or go on family vacations. In our house there is no such thing as Friday movie night with the kids. There will be no children to hold close, no character to build, and no little league games to attend to cheer for our little guy. We won't tuck them in, kiss them good night, or watch them sleep. We will not be parents.

✳ ✳ ✳

*Be anxious for nothing, but in everything by prayer
and supplication with thanksgiving let your requests
be made known to God. And the peace of God,
which surpasses all comprehension,
will guard your hearts and your minds
in Christ Jesus.*
—Philippians 4:6-7

✳ ✳ ✳

It is impossible to understand why some start their families so easily and for others it is so difficult. As we struggled with infertility, peace was the last thing I could find. Every time I saw a child being neglected or abused, I became angry. It didn't seem fair to me that a woman who did not want her children had several and that couples who prayed desperately for one child were denied.

As I read the words of Paul, I realized that my petition for a child might take a while, but the peace that takes me beyond my limited understanding was just waiting for me. My sanity was intact because of the peace of Christ within me.

It is easier to pray for what we want than it is to allow the answer to come in God's time rather than ours. As much as we knew that we would love our children, God loves us even more. As much as we would have done everything to protect our children, our Heavenly Father will protect His children too.

My nephew tried to run into the street one day. His goal was the ice cream shop on the other side. He knew the destination, and he knew how to get there. As I grabbed his arm to stop him, he protested.

"I know how to cross the street," he complained.

At that moment, the semi that had rounded the corner as he stepped off the curb passed in front of us.

"Oh—I didn't see that," he said.

We cannot see what's coming around the corner. Trusting God will never be detrimental to our lives.

Lord, our family is in your hands. Lead us to the doctors and procedures that are part of your plan for us. Help us to communicate with each other and to support one another throughout this journey. Help us rejoice with those who celebrate pregnancies and children during our time of barrenness. We will trust you to walk with us. In Jesus' name. Amen.

2
MISCARRIAGE, MISDIAGNOSIS, AND MISSION IMPOSSIBLE

> *But He said, "The things impossible with people are possible with God."*
>
> —Luke 18:27

I was in my early thirties, and there was still time to have children as we had dreamed. We started researching to find the best infertility doctor in our area. There were several whom my primary care physician recommended. We felt blessed that we would be in touch with a miracle worker very soon. It could really happen this time. My hip had healed nicely, John and I had grown in our love for each other, and we were ready to try again.

Knowing our desire to proceed with conservative treatments, our new doctor started a series of Clomid at our first visit. We prayed that it would work, but we left our options open. It was a new century, a new millennium; surely new therapies were just around the corner.

I spent every spare moment researching fertility treatments to determine our best options. There were a variety of hormone stimulators on the market, each with its own set of prerequisite diagnoses. Surgically assisted conception and artificial insemination were possibilities. We were still praying for a miracle with the Clomid but leaving our options open.

We decided against in vitro fertilization. The thought of having frozen embryos that might not ever develop into children felt wrong for us. To be honest, the financial requirement of in vitro was somewhat a factor that kept us from looking into it too deeply.

We kept praying and kept believing God would give us the desire of our hearts. We trusted Him to make our family complete.

The queasy mornings started the day my doctor went on vacation. Two pink lines put me on cloud nine, but I waited to tell John. I didn't want to hurt him again. I knew this time would be different. The queasy mornings were a welcome addition to my day. I woke up hoping to feel nauseated. A checklist of symptoms grew in my mind.

Lack of energy. *Check.*

Tiny sensations in my belly. *Check.*

Nausea. *Check.*

A new chapter in our life together was growing in me. It was all I could do to contain my excitement until I could see my doctor. His two-week vacation dragged on as my anticipation grew.

I was scheduled to be his first appointment when he returned from Greece. Until then, I kept my pink-lined stick in a zip-lock bag stashed in my top dresser drawer. I could hardly wait to show him and let his tests confirm what I already knew.

I didn't have much energy all day, but I had decided that would be normal for the next several months. After dinner, John went to relax in his recliner, and I went into my office to work on an article.

There was no sudden movement, no cramping. Warmth on my legs sent me dashing to the bathroom. It was seven feet from my desk, but by the time I had reached the tile floor there was already a trail of blood on the carpet. It would not stop—I was losing too much blood. Dizzy and scared, I yelled for John.

In the emergency room the hemorrhaging continued. A negative pregnancy test ruled out my self-diagnosed miscarriage. The list of possibilities was short but inconclusive until the doctors could stop the bleeding. My hemoglobin was dangerously low, less than seven. The nurse couldn't keep the warm blankets coming fast enough.

The doctor admitted me for monitoring while they dripped estrogen into my veins in an attempt to stop the bleeding. She cautiously released me the next morning, and a series of diagnostic tests was scheduled.

A suspicious ultrasound led to more tests. The doctor wanted to do a dilation and curettage (D&C)—a scraping to remove the contents of the uterus—and a biopsy. Since the bleeding had stopped, it was scheduled for two weeks later. All I could do in the meantime was rest.

I didn't make it to that appointment before the bleeding resumed. The doctor who was on call performed an emergency D&C, sending the tissue to the lab for the biopsy. The bleeding lessened after the procedure but didn't stop.

Even with the iron supplements I was taking, my hemoglobin count remained at seven. I was weak and tired. Fear took me on a journey through scenarios that left me drained and confused. Would I ever be able to give John a child? Why was this happening to us? What had I done to deserve this?

My ministry schedule was in full swing, and I didn't want to miss a beat. I repeated silently throughout the long days, "I can do all things through Christ who strengthens me" (Philippians 4:13, NKJV). I kept an attitude of victory and strength in front of the world. I knew my faith was strong, but I was beginning to feel like Job, sitting in the ashes of my dreams and scraping my festering heart with broken hopes.

My determination to put on a strong front served me well until I collapsed after a ministry planning meeting. As I stood up to leave, I lost focus of the room, my circulation seemed to pause, and suddenly I was resting in the arms of two friends who leaned in to catch me on the way to the floor.

I explained the reason for my fall and tried to brush it off, but my friends insisted I go to the emergency room. The familiar ER team quickly took blood, discovering my hemoglobin was even lower. Technicians rolled bags of A-positive on IV carts into my cubicle. Someone called John, but he was working a couple of hours from the hospital. He made some calls, and my friend Susan showed up as the transfusion started.

My appointment to find out biopsy results was still a week away, but I had to know. I asked the ER doctor if he could find my file in the system. Reluctantly, he agreed to check for me. When he disappeared for more than an hour, I knew what he was about to tell me. With Susan standing by my side, I heard the diagnosis that I never expected. The doctor averted his eyes as he said it: "You do have cancer."

There it was, the word no one wanted to say aloud. I had cancer. Immediately I felt safe. It didn't make sense, even to me. But I knew I was wrapped in the Holy Spirit and that no matter what was about to happen, I would not go through it alone.

I wonder what God is going to do with this, I thought. I laughed and cried at the same time.

The doctor offered to send someone to speak with me. "We have a counselor on call," he suggested. Thankfully, Susan understood and assured the doctor that I was fine. She immediately made phone calls to our prayer chain and our pastor.

I wanted to be fine. I wanted to know that God had a plan. I wanted to believe that everything was going to be okay for my family no matter what this diagnosis meant for my life.

There was talk about stages, but I didn't understand what that meant. The doctor said that the cancer was well differentiated. I didn't know what that meant either. I just knew that I could hardly wait to be home, away from all of this.

An appointment was scheduled with the doctor I had seen in the ER when this nightmare started. Susan drove me home in silence. Neither of us wanted to say that horrible word. She offered to stay with me until John got home from work, but I just wanted to be alone.

In the silence of the house, the doctor's words echoed through my head. *Cancer.* I knew at that moment that I would never give birth to a child. I would never know what it felt like to have a tiny person growing in my belly. I would never feel the kick of a tiny, newly formed foot. I shivered against the chill of the house on that late March evening and pulled the comforter over my grief. How could I tell John that he would never have a son?

I heard his truck pull into the driveway, but I couldn't move. He would be in the house soon enough. I didn't see any reason to greet him at the door with my news. I heard the door open and his boots on the kitchen floor. My grief magnified every sound.

Tears I had been pushing back flooded my eyes as he sat down on the bed. I reached for his hand and pulled myself toward the strength his arms offered. As he held me, I whispered the words that would change everything about our life. "I have cancer."

I didn't realize I was still holding the crumpled release form from the emergency room until I felt him pull it from my fingers. He read the doctor's scribbled notes. *Endometrial carcinoma—recommend follow-*

up with OB and oncologist. He dropped the paper onto the floor and held me.

"It's going to be okay." He attempted to reassure me, but he knew neither of us believed it. We lay silently in each other's arms and fell into a night of fitful sleep.

The next morning John asked the question I had not considered. "Are you going to die?"

"No, I don't think so." I couldn't stop my tears. I had not considered the fact that cancer could take my life. "But we won't have a baby." I sobbed as he pulled me to him again. He didn't say anything else.

Calling my mom was much harder than telling John. Her tears broke through the strength she tried to offer. Her little girl was almost two thousand miles away from her, with cancer. She said she would come to be with me for surgery or treatments, whatever I needed. We prayed and said goodbye, hoping for a miracle.

A few days later John and I sat in the doctor's office as she explained our options for treatment. Her recommendation was expected. A total hysterectomy including the ovaries was the best course of treatment. The tumor was the size of a plum but seemed to be encapsulated by the uterus. I would be okay as long as the cancer hadn't spread to the lymph system. Everything would be checked during surgery. Once they had the pathology findings, an oncologist would decide if I needed to undergo chemotherapy or radiation.

John pulled away from me as if I had a contagious disease. He closed his emotions behind mental walls and refused to let them out. He didn't want me to be hurt by his disappointment. Instead, he shut me out. I needed him more than ever. He needed to escape.

Having my mom with me during the surgery was more helpful than I could have imagined. She arrived the day before surgery and stayed by my side until I was home. John visited the hospital for a couple of minutes each day but always had a reason he had to leave quickly. I tried to understand his feelings, but I didn't.

My final diagnosis did not come until after my reproductive organs were removed. The cause of our infertility, the cause of rapid weight gain in my early twenties, and the cause of my cancer was one treatable syndrome that was never detected. Polycystic ovary syndrome (PCOS) had been raging in my body, leaving reproductive destruction in its path. I had most of the classic symptoms, yet no doctor had ever mentioned it to me before. If it had been identified early, there were treatments that could have resulted in pregnancy. Instead, it caused insulin resistance, slowed my metabolism, and caused hyperplasia of the uterus, resulting in the cancer.

My heartbreak changed to anger as I listened to my doctor talk about what could have been. Her words stung my throat like acid coming from the pit of my stomach. I wanted to scream at the doctors who had said there was nothing wrong. I wanted them to tell me why they didn't know what was wrong with me years before. I was angry with every doctor I had seen since childhood. Why hadn't they found the problem sooner?

❋ ❋ ❋

John . . .

Pamela had been acting strangely for a while. I wondered if she was going through some kind of hormonal changes, but I knew better than to ask if her mood swings were related to anything remotely female. I thought maybe it was just the stress from discussing a baby again.

Pamela had never had a normal period. I had seen her skip months, and I had seen her bleed for sixty days. The night she started hemorrhaging, I thought it was just another weird period. I should have listened when she said something was wrong. I didn't. I was shocked that she lost so much blood that night. I felt terrible that I didn't believe her.

When she told me about the cancer, I didn't know what to do. I could not fix it for her. I couldn't give her the children that she wanted more than anything, and I couldn't stand the thought of losing my wife. She had all the faith in the world that we would have children, yet there she was, having her dreams ripped from her own body. We had been faithful. What kind of God lets this happen to a woman who has been so faithful to Him? Her faith was the reason I learned to trust God. I wasn't sure I could keep trusting. She just kept saying through her tears that God had a reason.

"Okay, tell me, God," I challenged. "What could possibly be the reason?"

Every hope she had to carry our children was gone. Nothing I could say would change things for her, for us. Therefore, I just stopped saying anything. I didn't want to hurt her more by talking about my feelings over our permanent childlessness. I was thankful that her mom was here during her surgery. It saved me from having to know what to say.

More than anything, I was afraid for her. What if they didn't get all the cancer? What if it came back? Her medical insurance at work hadn't kicked in yet. How were we going to pay for the treatments she needed?

I just wanted everything to be okay. I wanted Pamela to be healthy, and I wanted our life back the way it was before this nightmare started.

❖ ❖ ❖

Pamela . . .

Polycystic ovary syndrome is a rather mysterious health problem that can affect a woman's menstrual cycle, causes infertility, changes hormone levels, and can affect the heart, blood vessels, and physical appearance. PCOS also causes insulin resistance, changing the way the body processes sugar. Although a link to diabetes has not been proven, women with PCOS often develop Type-2 diabetes. Insulin resistance causes the metabolism to slow, resulting in rapid weight gain and abnormal difficulty losing weight.

Irregularity in the menstrual cycle can cause hyperplasia of the uterus. With this hyperplasia, the likelihood of developing cancer in the endometrial lining increases. The longer the condition goes undiagnosed, the greater the risk to the woman.

PCOS is not uncommon. Up to ten percent of women are affected by this condition. It is the most common cause of female infertility. Along with infertility, other symptoms of PCOS include obesity, typically with an apple shape; dark hair on the face, chest, back, or thighs, caused by high levels of male hormones called androgens; velvety patches of skin a couple of shades darker than normal under the arms, at the waistline, or on the upper thigh; and acne even into adulthood.

Researchers don't know the cause of PCOS. However, most agree that more than one factor may play a role in the development of the condition. Some genetic links have been established. Women with PCOS often have a mother or sister with the same condition; studies are still being conducted to establish heredity of PCOS. Some studies also link insulin levels to PCOS, but experts are still waffling about whether PCOS causes insulin resistance or whether being insulin resistant promotes the occurrence of PCOS.[1]

While PCOS is the most common, accounting for seventy-five percent of all cases of anovulatory infertility,[2] there are many other reasons that a couple may not be able to conceive. It is important to be prepared to ask questions, even at your first appointment with an infertility specialist.

Ovulatory disorders are one of the most common reasons women are unable to conceive. They account for about thirty percent of fertility disorders; however, approximately seventy percent of these cases can be successfully treated by the use of drugs such as Clomiphene. The causes of failed ovulation range from hormonal problems, scarred ovaries, and premature menopause to follicle problems.

Damage to the Fallopian tubes attributes to approximately twenty-five percent of female infertility. Tubal damage can be caused by infection, abdominal disease such as appendicitis and colitis, previous surgeries, ectopic pregnancies, and congenital defects in tubal development.

Endometriosis affects about ten percent of infertile couples. Endometriosis affects six to seven percent of all women. Of these, thirty to forty percent of patients with endometriosis are infertile. The symptoms most often linked to endometriosis include heavy, painful, and long periods, urinary urgency, rectal bleeding, and premenstrual spotting. Sometimes, however, no symptoms occur at all.

At least ten percent of female infertility is caused by an abnormal uterus. Fibroid cysts, polyps, and adenomyosis can cause obstructions between the uterus and Fallopian tubes. Congenital abnormalities, such as septate uterus, may lead to recurrent miscarriages or the inability to conceive.

Less common, and fairly easy to treat, are problems with cervical mucus. This mucus must be a certain consistency to allow sperm to swim easily within it. Hormone imbalances, like too little estrogen or too much progesterone, can cause this problem, which accounts for about three percent of infertility issues in women.[3]

✳ ✳ ✳

If you are struggling with infertility, leave no stone unturned. Make a list of anything about your body that does not seem normal.

The little things you might think are not important now could turn out to be very important later.

I had many of the symptoms of PCOS, but because I removed the facial hair, the doctor never noticed and didn't ask. I gained weight in my early twenties and had not been successful at shedding the extra pounds. My weight was proportioned evenly, atypical of the apple shape common in PCOS, so doctors did not see the connection. My menstrual cycle had been irregular and erratic since I was sixteen; still no one mentioned PCOS. I never heard of it until it was too late. I didn't know what questions to ask. When we began our journey through infertility in the 1990s, access to the Internet was still considered a luxury. Googling "infertility" to search for a cause was a foreign concept.

You must learn to be your own advocate in the mysterious world of medical infertility. Today there are tools and research at our fingertips. Use that to your advantage. You should not self-diagnose, but you do need to educate yourself enough to raise questions with your doctor. Don't worry about offending the doctor with too many questions. It is your right as a patient to receive the best possible care. You are advocating not only for your health but for your possible future children as well.

Choosing a Specialist

- Ask your primary care physician for a couple of recommendations.
- Check with the American Medical Association (AMA) or your state's medical board for disciplinary action taken against the doctor.
- Make an initial consultation appointment and interview with the doctor. Bring a list of your questions and concerns so you don't forget anything.
- Check on the reputation of the school from which the doctor received his or her degree. Include additional training and certifications.
- Ask for references. The doctor will not be able to disclose someone else's information but will often have patients who are willing to call you to give a reference.

Ultimately, you are in charge of your care. Don't be afraid to ask a lot of questions. If the doctor is put off by inquiries, that's a good indicator that you won't be happy with your care. Find out what continuing education the doctor has taken in the field of infertility. When a good doctor-patient relationship is established, you should be comfortable with your treatment. If not, seek a second opinion.

❊ ❊ ❊

I will lift up my eyes to the mountains; From whence shall my help come? My help comes from the LORD, Who made heaven and earth. He will not allow your foot to slip; He who keeps you will not slumber. Behold, He who keeps Israel will neither slumber nor sleep.
—Psalm 121:1-4

❊ ❊ ❊

Honestly, it is often a momentary relief to receive a diagnosis that explains infertility. Knowing why makes it easier to move toward figuring out what to do next. Accepting the diagnosis and moving forward does not negate your faith. Having faith in God as your ultimate healer and authority does not mean you can't or shouldn't take full advantage of medical science.

While you are going through medical procedures and treatments, you need to get adequate rest. You do not have to worry about what's going on while you sleep, because God does not sleep. He is constantly watching over you and providing for you. You can trust Him. He cares about every detail in your life. He sees your tears even when no one else seems to notice. He will bring comfort when you are frightened, peace when you are frustrated, and provision when you are empty.

Scripture tells us that God is not the author of confusion but of peace (1 Corinthians 14:33). He is the author and finisher of our faith. Our faithfulness to Christ during life's toughest times polishes our faith and builds our relationship with the Lord. Immerse yourself in scripture and prayer during the battle with infertility. Let the presence of the Lord soothe stress and weariness from the long road you have been traveling.

Lord, we know you are our healer. Thank you for being with us on this journey. God, we ask you for healing. We ask you to open the womb and allow a child to be delivered into our home. God, we know that you are omnipotent. We want your plan for our life. Give us peace and patience to follow you in all things. Let us remember to lift up our eyes to your will. In Jesus' name we pray. Amen.

3 IS ADOPTION AN OPTION?

Having the first fruits of the Spirit, even we ourselves groan within ourselves, waiting eagerly for our adoption as sons, the redemption of our body.

—Romans 8:23

An appointment with the oncologist resulted in a few days in the hospital to receive radiation implants. It was the best way to ensure that there would not be a recurrence of the cancer.

I spent four days in a sterile room completely alone. Visitors could stay only a few minutes a day because of the risk of radiation exposure. It would be harder to see John for a few minutes and then say goodbye, so we talked on the phone. Conversations were short, because neither of us knew what to say. Even the nurses stayed in the room for only a few minutes at a time. Lead shields were positioned strategically around the bed for the safety of hospital staff. I joked about being radioactive, but inside I wasn't laughing.

Recovery from surgery and radiation took several weeks. I had a lot of time to peruse the Internet. I wanted to learn everything I could about adoption before I presented the idea to John. We hadn't really discussed it much, because we had always hoped we would be able to have our children biologically. I mentioned it casually one evening, but he said we should wait until I was feeling better to discuss it. I agreed to wait, but I didn't want to wait too long.

I looked up every private adoption agency and foster parenting program in the state and requested their information packets. Each envelope was stuffed with pages of information on eligible children just waiting for a home and parents to love them. They were such amazing children. I fell in love with beautiful newborns, chubby-cheeked toddlers, wide-eyed preschoolers, and even a few preteens. I never imagined there were so many children who needed love from families like ours. I was convinced that these children were the reason we could not have our own.

I knew John was disappointed that I couldn't give him the son he wanted. Adoption seemed like the perfect solution. We could choose a son. I was relieved that John could have the desire of his heart. I could hardly wait to share the agencies and pictures with him. I chose the ones I preferred and arranged everything in a notebook.

That night John came home to a special dinner. He knew something was up, but he played along and enjoyed the game. I waited until he had some time to relax before I brought out the notebook.

"I've been researching adoption," I said as I eagerly handed him the book. "I think we should get started right away." My eagerness was met with a blank stare.

John took the book and began thumbing through the pages I had so carefully selected. His expression changed slightly with each child's picture. I couldn't tell if it was sadness or fear, but it was not what I had expected.

"I know it's expensive, but so is having a baby naturally." I found myself talking faster than usual, trying to explain why adoption would be so perfect for us. "Look at that little girl. Isn't she cute?" I wasn't sure if he nodded or rolled his eyes, so I continued. "We would be such perfect parents, and these kids are just waiting for homes." I paused for a breath and continued. "These kids need parents who love the Lord. They deserve to know how much they are loved. Life in the country is perfect for them." My reasons to adopt were endless. John listened to my plea for a child and to all my justifications for jumping headlong into the process.

"So what do you think?" I asked, ready for his approval of my plan.

He closed the notebook. "I'm not buying a kid." His answer was flat. He got up from the table and went to the living room. Remote in his hand, he leaned back in his chair.

I followed him, trying to understand his reaction. "Adoption is not buying a kid." My voice was shaking as I tried to stay calm and rational.

"I know you want to be a mother. I wanted our child too. It didn't happen. Maybe God knows I wouldn't be a good father." I tried to argue, but he wasn't finished. "I don't think I could commit the rest of my life to someone else's child." He was calm as he spoke. "I don't want to take a child who has already had a rough time and make it worse for them."

I did not understand why he thought he couldn't love a child who didn't have his DNA. He was always loving and affectionate with nieces and nephews. We headed the children's ministry at our church, and he was great with those kids. We even had one special-needs child in our church, and he was often the only adult who could handle him.

Nothing I said would change his mind. I retreated to the kitchen as he clicked the remote to find a Western on television. Tears stung my eyes as I cleared the dishes and leftovers from the table. I replayed everything in my head. How could he say no to those beautiful faces? John had the most tender heart I had ever seen. Sure—he put up walls to hide his emotions sometimes, but I understood that. He had learned it from his father. I had to find a way to break through his resistance. The only thing I knew for sure was to pray.

I prayed as I cleaned the kitchen, hoping for an answer before the dishes were dry. "Why does this have to be so hard?" I wanted to yell at God. I wanted Him to know how much this was hurting me. I needed to be a mother. We needed to be parents. I didn't care if my body produced the child or not. The love God placed in our marriage had to be for something, for some purpose, for someone.

I prayed for an opportunity to adopt through some other avenue, something that John would see clearly as God's plan. I read story after story of miraculous adoptions that just fell into the laps of childless couples. I wanted to be one of those stories. I just had to wait on God. I was confident that He had a plan for our life.

We had worked with teens at a camp for underprivileged kids for a few summers. Maybe our child was going to come from a young girl who needed to find a home for her baby. I was grasping at every possibility that would make John see the future the way I did.

* * *

The day I met Annette I thought the tables of childlessness were turning. I was working on the newsletter for the camp. Annette walked into the office carrying a baby girl. Chloe was five months old. She had a ton of curly brown hair and big green eyes. She was probably one of the prettiest babies I had ever seen. Annette couldn't have been more than eighteen years old.

"I don't know what to do, and some girls at the Laundromat said you might be able to help me." She was trembling and close to tears as she spoke. "My baby is hungry, and I don't have anything for her." She continued to tell her story. "I don't think I can take care of her anymore."

I listened to her story—a young, single mother with no support. She didn't have any money and had been staying with whatever friends would let her borrow their couch.

I made a call, borrowed a car seat, and we headed to town. We bought formula, diapers, and rice cereal—and a cute little outfit to replace the stained pajamas Chloe was wearing when they arrived at the camp.

Annette was grateful for the assistance, but there was still something on her mind. "Would you be able to watch Chloe for the weekend?" Her question caught me off guard, even though I had envisioned that scenario in my mind. I had known her less than four hours, and she was asking me to care for her child.

"I know you probably think that's too much, but if I could just have a couple of days to think without having to take care of her, it would help me a lot."

She continued to explain her situation, but I wasn't listening. I was already planning how I could explain this miracle to John. I was sure that having a weekend of freedom would make Annette realize that she needed to find a home for Chloe.

We arranged for Annette to meet me at the Laundromat on Sunday night to pick up Chloe. For the next forty-eight hours, I thought of what it would be like to be her mother.

John was not excited about having a stranger's baby in the house. He was concerned that I had taken Chloe in without questioning the girl who would so readily leave an infant with a stranger. He thought I should call Child Protective Services. I talked him out of that idea. If this was the child God had for us, it was better to keep her out of the system if possible. "If Annette decides we should keep her, then we can just go through a lawyer—there's no need to involve the state." I guess I was convincing, because he didn't say anything else.

Annette was sitting on the counter in the Laundromat when I walked in with Chloe on Sunday evening. As soon as she saw us, she jumped up and ran to Chloe. The look of love in her eyes told me she was not going to hand her beautiful baby girl to anyone.

Annette had used her time to call her parents in Springfield. They were on the way to pick them up. She was taking Chloe and going home. Her parents were going to help her with Chloe so that she could go back to school and make a life for her child.

I should have been happy for them. I couldn't. I was heartbroken. I felt like a cruel joke had just been played on my heart. I didn't understand how God could let me get my hopes up by letting me actually hold and care for this little one for a while.

John resisted the urge to say that he had told me so, but I knew he was wondering how far I was willing to go to get a child. I wanted to be a mother. I didn't care if it made sense. I didn't care if it was going to take every penny we had.

"Maybe God isn't going to give us a child," John said, too matter-of-factly for me.

"God would not give me such a strong desire to parent if he wasn't going to fulfill that desire." I argued.

We were having the same argument too often. He knew it was pointless to try to convince me to give up. I didn't understand how John could be so rational about everything. I knew he wanted me to be happy. It would have taken so little, just a miracle—just a child.

A friend suggested that I introduce John to the foster parent program. I had resisted that idea, because I wasn't sure I could care for a child and then give him or her back to parents who had been abusive or neglectful. It could be a way to adopt without buying a child and without wishing for a baby in a basket to show up on the porch. I talked to John. He agreed to explore the options. I made an appointment with child services.

John didn't show up for the appointment. I rescheduled three times, and three times something came up that prevented him from making it. The social worker suggested that John and I weren't on the same page about children. I didn't want to hear her judging my marriage. She said that not every childless couple should adopt. "Some people just aren't made for it," she said. "Maybe you should just let it go."

I walked out of her office in tears. My last hope to become a mother had just told me to let it go. I was angry. She had children. She had no idea what it was like to have so much love to give with no one to receive it.

I was still crying when John came home. I thought he would retreat to his recliner and the remote as he usually did. Instead, he came into the kitchen where I was cooking supper. He didn't say anything; he just put his arms around my waist and held me. I leaned back to feel the support he offered. Tears still poured from my eyes, but now they weren't tears of anger and frustration. Suddenly I wasn't alone. John turned me toward him and wiped my face with his shirt. He kissed my forehead and pulled me into a long embrace.

"It's going to be okay," he whispered. "God does have a plan, but you have to let Him reveal it. We can't make it happen."

I knew he was right. I wanted to argue, but there was nothing to say that could refute the fact that God is sovereign. I had to let go. Letting go was the last thing I wanted to do. I couldn't understand how God could plan for us to remain childless. I couldn't understand what I had done to deserve this sentence. If God's plan for my life was not to be a mother, I wanted to know what it was. Nothing made sense.

❊ ❊ ❊

John . . .

I was so relieved that she was going to be all right. The doctor told us that with radiation there was less than a one-percent chance the cancer would reoccur. That was great news. I knew she was heartbroken over the finality of not having children, but I hoped that she would just settle into our life together. We could do many things if we didn't have kids. I decided to think about the unseen benefits. Pamela had taught me about trusting God, but now it didn't seem as if she trusted anyone or anything except her desire to be a mother.

When she suggested adoption, I wasn't sure how to react. I wanted to say yes. I wanted her to be happy, and I wondered if an adopted child was right for us. It also scared me. The idea of loving and raising my own child seemed much different from taking on the responsibility of another man's child—a child that he either didn't want or couldn't care for. I knew that this decision was the most important I would ever make. I had considered the idea of adoption from the moment we lost our baby. But when she brought out the notebooks, I realized how much the idea did not appeal to me.

I prayed and asked God to show me what to do. I never had peace with the idea of committing to an adopted child for the rest of my life. I had a co-worker who adopted a little boy because his wife wanted to. Ten years later, he resented the boy for taking his wife's time and her heart. I didn't think I would be like that man, but I wasn't sure. What if I was? I couldn't stand the thought that I might resent the thing that we wanted most.

With so much confusion in my heart, I decided to say no. If God wanted us to have children through adoption, he would have to place that desire in my heart. I couldn't help the way I felt, and it wouldn't have been fair to agree, no matter how much it hurt to deny Pamela the one thing she said she needed to be happy. I prayed for God to change my heart. As time went on, I was more certain that this wasn't going to happen.

❈ ❈ ❈

Adoption is a wonderful way for childless couples to build the family they desire. It can be one of the most rewarding forms of parenting. Infertile couples spend years waiting for a child who matches their criteria and for whom they fill the requirements set by the birth parents or adoption agency. Many couples have paid a high fee and gone through home studies, background checks, and thick stacks of paperwork only to have their hopes dashed when a birth mother changes her mind.

❈ ❈ ❈

Jenny felt the baby kick and rolled her eyes. She could hardly wait to get through the next three months. Her social worker told her all about the family they found for her baby. They were good people—churchgoers, from what Jenny could tell. They were in their thirties and didn't have any children of their own. Adoption was the only way they would ever have a child. At nineteen, Jenny felt that she was doing something good by giving her baby to a couple who could love him completely. *Maybe,* she thought, *this will make up for the bad things I've done.* The baby kicked again, and she knew she was in for a long night.

Over the next three months Jenny did everything she was supposed to do for the baby and for her health. She admitted that she was getting used to the active baby's antics in the middle of the night, and by her thirty-sixth week she looked forward to feeling him move. She didn't know for sure the baby was a boy, but she imagined with the athletics going on in her belly that this baby would be a football star.

Ken and Donna waited anxiously for the delivery of their baby. The adoption agency assured them that the mother was a healthy young lady. She was clean and came from a good family. When she found out she was pregnant, her first thought was to give her child the chance to have a good life. She knew she was too young to be a mother. This adoption was the best choice for everyone, a win-win situation from the start.

Labor pains started early in the evening, but Jenny knew she had several hours before they would be close enough to go to the hospital. She called her social worker so that her baby's family would know he was on his way. She didn't want him to be without his new parents for even a moment.

Several hours later, Jenny gave birth to a son. He was twenty-two inches long and had lots of thick blonde hair. It was curly like Jenny's, and his chin already mirrored hers. She was going to hold him for only a moment. She just wanted to explain that she loved him and that giving him away was better for him. As she kissed his forehead, Jenny breathed in deeply so she would never forget the fragrance of her firstborn. It was time to hand him back to the nurse. As her son left the room, swaddled in blue flannel receiving blankets, a piece of her heart went with him.

At the nursery window Ken and Donna stared at the baby boy they had waited for such a long. There were some papers that had to be signed by his biological mother, and then their little family would be going home. A couple of home visits and a court date would make everything legal. Their life was finally going to be complete.

Jenny woke up to find her social worker next to the bed smiling at her. Pulling the table toward Jenny, she handed her the papers that would give her baby to his new family. Jenny held the pen at the edge of the signature line and watched tears fall on the contract before her. "I can't do it," she sobbed. "I can't give my baby away."

Jenny pushed the table away and sobbed into her hands. She did not want to hurt anyone, but she couldn't bear to give up the life she helped to create.

Ken and Donna were devastated. Everything they had done in the past several months in preparation for their new arrival was in vain. The process would have to start again.

Financially strained and emotionally devastated, Ken and Donna decided to wait before they requested another child. For Donna, the emotional roller coaster was more than she wanted to experience on a regular basis.

✳ ✳ ✳

The fees for a domestic or interstate adoption average $8,000 to $15,000, according to American Adoptions, a private adoption agency founded on the belief that lives of children can be bettered through adoption. Foster parenting and state-run agencies can make the process less expensive. There are adoption programs in all fifty states, the District of Columbia, and five territories. Fees to adopt through the Foster Parent Programs in the United States vary. Some states absorb the entire cost of these adoptions. In other states, adoptive parents can expect to pay up to $5,000 in processing and legal fees. Even the foster programs cannot guarantee placement or expedition of the adoption process. Couples wait years to get the call that their baby is ready to come home.

Chris and Glenda King tried to conceive a child for two-and-a-half years when they were told it was unsafe to have a child due to medication she had to take. A hysterectomy a short time later forced the Kings to look at alternatives.

When they decided to adopt, they expected to have a child immediately. "We had no idea how long it would take," said Glenda. "We thought that once we decided to move forward we would be able to select a child."

The Kings were so excited at the prospect of having a baby that they decorated the nursery and prepared their home for the new arrival. It took more than two years before anything started to happen with their adoption process. "Walking past that room was a constant reminder that we still didn't have a child," Glenda said. "It was heart-wrenching to face the empty crib on a daily basis." Glenda was ready to give up after many months of disappointment.

In January 1994 a phone call from her mother, a strong prayer warrior, gave her a glimmer of hope. "This is going to be the year, Glenda," she assured her. "You will get your baby this year." Glenda and Chris wanted to believe that was true.

In May, Glenda's grandmother, also a woman of strong faith, called Glenda's sister and told her that God knew their request and that it was okay to let it go and let God work. She didn't want to tell Glenda. She didn't want her to face more disappointment, just in case.

The year was almost over, and Glenda had accepted the fact that they might never get a baby. As they drove to a Christmas party on December 18, Glenda was feeling darker than she ever had. Emotion overwhelmed her, and she was in tears by the time they pulled into their friend's driveway. Chris tried to console her, but her tears would not be stopped. They left the party and went home.

The following Tuesday Glenda took her niece and nephew with her to work. They enjoyed helping her wrap presents for the residents of the nursing home. She was enjoying her time with the kids and was beginning to feel a little more Christmas spirit. When she answered her page to a telephone call, her emotional roller coaster started again. It was her worker from the Department of Family Services. "What is your company policy on maternity leave?" Glenda's heart jumped into her throat. "I just need to know to update your file," the caseworker explained. "This doesn't mean anything. It's just a formality."

The joyful mood that almost snuck into Glenda's mind was gone. She needed a break. Taking the kids out to lunch provided enough of a distraction that Glenda thought she might be able to make it through the rest of the day.

When she returned to work, there was a message from her case-worker. Glenda didn't want to talk to her again that day, but she obediently returned the call.

"I needed to finish the paperwork, and I didn't want to say anything until I knew it would happen." Her voice was filled with excitement. "Glenda, there is a little girl available now. How soon can you get here?"

Glenda could not believe what she was hearing. With tears of joy streaming down her face, she flew out the door and drove straight to the Department of Family Services office. Chris met her there. As soon as they saw the beautiful seven-day-old baby, they fell in love with her. On December 22, 1994, Emylee Myranda came home for Christmas.

In 2000, the Kings added to their family through the adoption of Elijah.

Adoption serves several important purposes in contemporary American society. It is a way for individuals and couples to form a legal parental relationship with a non-biological child. As such, it benefits children whose birth parents are unable or unwilling to raise them and provides adults who are unable to conceive or carry a pregnancy to term a means to bring children into their families. Adoption is also used to legalize the parental relationship between a de facto parent and a non-biological child, such as a stepchild, a foster child, or a child of a relative, for whom they are already providing care on a daily basis.[1]

It seems like the easy answer. Just tell someone that you are infertile, and their automatic response is "Oh, well—you can always adopt." It is the most helpful thing most people can think of to say when faced with a friend's tragic news of childlessness. It is also one of the most hurtful things to hear. "You can always adopt" implies that it is a simple process—as if adoption is like going to Wal-Mart. Boy babies on aisle three, girls on aisle twelve, select your option package at customer service, where you can choose from curly red hair, the blue-eyed blonde, or a bright brunette package. It sounds ridiculous, and that is how it feels to the childless couple who has heard that phrase every day for years.

Not every couple is called to adopt. It is an emotional, often expensive, and grueling process. While there are very few adoptive parents who would take back even one moment of the journey, the outcome is not always happy. Parents who are not called to the ministry of adoption may find themselves emotionally spent. In rare cases, it reflects in their parenting of adopted children, resulting in life-changing trauma for the child.

The Bible instructs believers to care for orphans. That would seem to indicate that adoption is not only a good way to build a family but is also actually required. Adoption of orphans seems to be an explanation for couples who find themselves unable to bear children biologically.

As John and I struggled with decisions about adoption, that theory frightened me. Was John leading us into disobedience? I knew there were no doors into adoption flying open for us, but it still did not take much goading from well-meaning people in our church to make me feel guilty for not actively pursuing adoption. The fact that I didn't understand why God seemed to deny me the baby I was praying for added to my guilt.

Using the scriptures regarding orphans and widows to heap condemnation on the heads of the childless is not only cruel but also a misuse of scripture. The mandate usually quoted is in the Book of James: "Pure and undefiled religion in the eyes of our God and Father is this: to visit the orphans and widows in their distress, and to keep oneself unstained by the world" (James 1:27).

Other scripture discusses justice for orphans (Deuteronomy 10:18) and defending orphans (Isaiah 1:17). There are many ways to support orphans besides adoption. Volunteering in a shelter, working in orphanages on missions trips, sending money to reliable organizations that feed, clothe, and educate orphaned children around the world, and donating time or items to local service organizations are all valuable ways to help those in need, including orphans.

The words of a missionary I heard when I was a child still reverberate in my mind. "Not everyone is called to the mission field," he said. "Some are called to be the senders." The same admonishment applies to adoption. Some are called to be adoptive parents; others are called to give in other ways. If you are one of the couples called to adoption, then you should absolutely be obedient to that calling. But if you are not called to adopt, it's okay to say no.

Social pressure, feelings of inadequacy, and childless stigmas should not be your motivation to adopt a child. If they are, please reconsider. Wait until you are certain you are ready to make a lifelong commitment. For better or worse, no matter what baggage they might bring, no matter what behavior, illness, or difficulty presents itself, adopted children are your *real* children. There is no turning back.

Deciding that we would not pursue adoption was the most difficult decision we ever made. Both of us had to be ready to make the commitment. We were not. John was honest about his state of mind from the beginning. He wasn't sure adoption was something he could do, and he was not afraid to say so.

I, on the other hand, was convinced that I had to be a mother through whatever means available. It took me a while to look at my motives without bias. Being honest about your motivation and your level of commitment will save you and your potential child from pain in the future.

My friend Vicki Sprouse has agonized publicly about deciding whether or not to adopt.

One Sunday in church we sat behind a couple several years older than us. They had adopted a child who appeared to be of Latino heritage. I heard the woman talking to someone about it. I don't know if they were previously unable to conceive or if they had chosen not to have children, but after thirty years of marriage, they had just adopted a two-and-a-half-year-old.

Their adorable toddler was playing quietly in the pew. Her sweet whispers brought tears to my eyes. Suddenly the desire to adopt, which I thought was gone, came crashing back on me.

I didn't know if my fresh desire to adopt was coincidental happenstance, or if it was God trying to tell me something. After two near misses with adoption several years earlier following arduous years of infertility treatments, my heart could take no more.

For our emotional well-being, we had stopped and had not pursued it further. Our financial situation was also favorable for adoption. But it's important to remember that whether you do it privately, closed, domestic, or internationally, adoption is a costly process.

Those who have not gone through the process seem to think you can just walk into a church, pick out a kid, and leave with your child the same day. Those days, like the orphan train that made a simple system of adoption necessary, are long gone.

I sat there praying, not knowing if my renewed desire was from God or simply a desire that I harbored because it was the only thing left we could do to obtain a child of our own. I wondered if this new longing was fleeting or if it was going to take root and grip my heart with more pain.

I believe adoption is a calling. I don't think that it should be done for self-serving reasons, such as providing a grandchild for aging parents, filling a social void, or so others will see what a good person you are to take in that poor child. Adoption should come from a place of love that will benefit the child and fulfill a God-ordained place in your heart. The joy and blessing that comes from parenting should be a collateral benefit from overflowing love.

In the past this desire has waxed and waned. I know that if we are supposed to adopt, God will have to work miraculously. First, my husband and I need to be on the same page. My husband is content with our life, and so am I most of the time. Neither of us believes, at this point, that we are supposed to adopt, but that does little to squelch the desire in my heart when it shows up.

If we both felt the leading of the Lord toward adoption, God would have to do some major door-opening. I have no doubt if God's plan includes children for us, He will not be limited by our circumstances. That's the side of me that contains faith the size of a mustard seed, a very tiny mustard seed. Nonetheless, my faith tells me to be open and available to whatever God opens up for us.

My truest desire is to be obedient to God. I don't want to miss His best for me, for my marriage, or for a potential child He might place in our life.

The attitude that Vicky shares in her story is the same lesson the Lord showed me in my darkest moment. It is not about our goals, our dreams, or our desires. In light of eternity, the thing that matters most is our willingness to submit ourselves to the lordship of Christ. It is

His desire to walk in close relationship with us that can bring things into perspective for us.

Sometimes walking close to the Lord brings the answers we hope for. But not every story of adoption is easy—not everyone has the finances, the strength, or the stamina to survive the process. If you enter the world of adoption, be ready to hold on for the entire ride.

✻ ✻ ✻

Dawn knew from the time she was a young girl that she would not have biological children. A rare ovarian disease took her reproductive organs before she started kindergarten.

"It wasn't a devastating realization to know that I was not going to have a baby," she said. "It was never an option for me in the first place. My dreams of having a family never included becoming pregnant."

When Sam Riley, the love of her life, asked her to marry him, he knew she could not have children. That did not stop their plans for a family.

"Our planning was different than a lot couples," she said. "Instead of discussing how many children we wanted, we talked adoption and surrogacy. We decided there was no reason our children couldn't belong to my husband biologically, just because I had no eggs."

With that in mind, surrogacy seemed to be the best option. Dawn's best friend and college roommate offered to carry a child for them. Kelly's generosity seemed like the perfect answer.

The Rileys located donated eggs from an egg donation program. Doctors harvested sperm from Sam. In the laboratory the donor eggs were fertilized and prepared for implantation in Kelly's uterus. Five embryos waited in cryogenic safety for their day of implantation.

The team attempted insemination four times without success. The fourth attempt resulted in a pregnancy, but Kelly miscarried within a few weeks. Heartbroken, they decided to look at adoption. They began working on inspections and paperwork with the State of California, still hoping for a miracle.

The Rileys' plan for their children to be biologically connected to their father was fading before their eyes. If the last embryo did not successfully attach in the uterus of their surrogate, Sam would be forced to give up his dream of a son who shared his genetic makeup.

The adoption process was starting to look like an excellent option. Home inspections were passed, classes were taken. Things were moving forward at a pace that finally brought hope. It seemed unreal to Dawn that she would soon be a mother.

At the same time, the final surrogacy procedure was underway. When the call came saying Stacey was pregnant with their child, Dawn and her husband were amazed. Still, they didn't stop the adoption proceedings for fear the pregnancy would end in another miscarriage.

Through their attorney, the Rileys found a young girl who was looking for a home for her child. Paperwork was drawn up, and in a few months their son was born. Matthew Allen was a beautiful baby with thick, dark hair. They fell in love with him the moment the saw him. They still had to go through a waiting period and official paperwork to finalize the adoption, but their oldest son was home.

Two months later Kelly gave birth to Sam's biological son. They were overjoyed by the fact that they had two children after being unsure they would ever have one.

The Rileys were thrilled. Benjamin was perfect, except that a rare genetic condition caused his retinas to detach easily. Even crying too hard could cause a hemorrhage in his eyes. Several trips to the emergency room caused personnel to alert child protective services. The Rileys found themselves under suspicion for shaking their baby.

The claim was unsubstantiated, and Benjamin was never taken from his home, but Matthew was removed temporarily, pending investigation. The adoption process stopped cold, and the Rileys' world began falling apart. Sam blamed himself for insisting that their child be biologically connected to his genes. He was completely unaware that he carried the gene for this condition that would eventually result in Benjamin being permanently blind.

Fighting the system that was burying their family while caring for their son, whose eyes continued to rupture, wore them down to the point of defeat. If it weren't for their faith and the determination to save their children, the Rileys would have given up. They didn't.

After several months of random home visits, court dates, and legal fees, the state released their case, allowing adoption proceedings to move forward. An adoption that should have been final in six months took more than two years to complete. Of course, to the Rileys it was just a technicality that made Matthew their son on paper. In their hearts, he was their child from day one.

While the Rileys are not facing permanent childlessness, their story could have ended in an adoption disaster. By God's grace they had the strength to push forward. The expenses they have faced during their quest for children are staggering.

They realize how blessed they are. "If I could tell someone who is considering adoption what to expect, it would be the unexpected," Dawn said. "There was nothing I could have imagined that would have prepared me for the battle we fought to bring Matthew home."

❊ ❊ ❊

For many families, adoption or surrogacy are perfect solutions to childlessness. Reports of thousands of children who need loving families are true. But not every family is called to adopt. If either partner is not ready to invest his or her heart in the process or is not capable of loving a child who is not biological offspring, *stop!*

John's refusal to consider adoption was the most difficult thing that has happened for me in our marriage. We have endured many things in eighteen years, but the idea that he found himself incapable of loving an innocent child almost changed my heart toward him. In retrospect, it was the best thing he could have done for our marriage. His willingness to be honest, even when it made him look bad, and even when I absolutely didn't want to hear him, saved us from more pain later.

It would have been easy for him to give in to my plea for a child. He is sweet and charming and would have, no doubt, passed the interview process with flying colors. But his motivation would have been to make our marriage better, not to complete our family.

There is a misconception that bringing children into your marriage makes everything better. While many of us realize how ludicrous that sounds, some believe a child is like the balm of Gilead to their marriage. Unfortunately, where there is already a break in character, putting a child in the mix can be disastrous for the marriage and devastating for the child.

Angelique was adopted at birth. Her adoptive parents couldn't have children, and their marriage was crumbling. Her adoptive mother could not bear the thought of not having children and promised she would be a better wife if she could be a mother. They decided to adopt, believing that having a child was all that was missing to make them happy.

Unfortunately, Angelique's adoptive parents should have remained childless.

Her adoptive father began sexually molesting her while she was still in elementary school. When she was twenty-one, Angelique had developed ulcerative colitis, bulimia, and severe depression. A childhood that was supposed to be made better by adoption had been a torturous nightmare for her.

Afraid for her safety but desperate to change her life, Angelique pressed charges against the man who should have been her safe haven. He argued against incest charges because they were not related by blood and therefore, according to his thinking, there was nothing wrong with what he was doing. He conceded that she was too young but didn't consider that criminal. He eventually pled guilty and was sentenced to prison.

Angelique searched for her birth parents and located her families on both sides. She found the loving support she had always longed for. Her birth family values marriage and children. They are nurturing and kind.

Angelique survived. Through a strong relationship with the Lord, she is no longer depressed, her self-esteem has grown to healthy levels, and she has a good relationship with the family who thought they were doing the best thing for her when they handed her to strangers for a better life.

Angelique's story is an extreme case. Most adoptive parents love and nurture their children in a happy, safe home. However, if Angelique's adoptive parents had been completely honest with themselves before they made a life-long commitment to her, they may have decided against adoption for their family. Angelique will always wonder if her adoptive father's moral deficiency could have been detected by a more careful evaluation of his emotional and mental state at the time of the adoption.

I know that John and I would not have abused a child in our home the way Angelique's father did, but that does not mean it would have been wise for us to proceed with adoption. There are far less dramatic ways to abuse or neglect a child without intending harm. John's recognition of his inability to bond with another person was honest. No matter how much I didn't like it, his willingness to speak uncomfortable truth allowed God to work in our lives and in my heart.

Couples who decide to adopt will face considerable expense and time commitments. If adopting domestically, couples should be prepared to travel for the birth of the baby and stay until the baby is released from the hospital. If the birth state is different than the state the adoptive family resides in, the family must stay until the approval of the Interstate Compact on the Placement of Children (ICPC) has been granted, which may take up to two weeks.

Although all fifty states and seven United States territories have adoption programs, many people find the process daunting. Some couples simply feel called to pursue adoption outside the United States. Couples contemplating international adoption should carefully research the travel requirements for the countries from which they are considering adoption and should be prepared to travel to the country from which they are adopting and stay in that country for a period that could range from a few days to several weeks.

Many adopt children from China, Belarus, Russia, or other countries overseas. While the process is sometimes faster than domestic adoption, that is not always the case. International adoption is not without its own obstacles and red tape.

Tamara Clymer shared her struggle with infertility earlier. The Clymers have adopted their beautiful children internationally. It has not been glamorous or easy. Before considering the investment it takes in time and finances to bring a child home, make sure you are ready for the difficult road you can face abroad.

The Clymers decided to adopt their fourth child from Ukraine. After finding an agency with whom they felt comfortable, they began the paper chase. Once the dossier was complete with the home study, birth and marriage certificates, proof of home ownership, medical exams, criminal background checks, and many other documents, they filed their request to the government for permission to adopt internationally. That process took about six months.

Once everything in the United States was notarized and approved and their savings were in place, Tami and Shad sent their adoption portfolio to Ukraine. Then they waited.

It took four months for them to receive news of an appointment with the adoption officials in Kiev. They waited three more months for the actual appointment, at which they selected a little girl from the photographs of children.

The next step was to meet the child. Unfortunately, it isn't always that simple. That selection fell through, and the Clymers had to start again with the officials in Kiev. They never imagined what the next few weeks would bring.

That Monday morning dawned bright. While the outside world was cloudy, drippy, and dreary, inside we were excited. We had spent the last three days agonizing over a decision to visit a little boy eight hours away by train. After speaking with our pediatrician and doing hours of our own research, we decided we could handle the little guy's epilepsy diagnosis. We wanted to meet him.

Thirty minutes after telling our facilitator of our decision, he called back. A French couple had filed the paperwork that morning to adopt our little guy. We were too late.

While I was happy little Sergei would soon have a family of his own, it also meant we were out of options. We already had two referrals fall through, and while the government adoption specialist suggested another little boy to visit, she wouldn't let us review his file. We either had to take his referral or wait for a second appointment. We couldn't remember what the little guy looked like, let alone be able to tell you what his diagnoses were. So we chose a third option: we decided to go home.

The adoption process had been so long, so intense, so draining that was taking everything I had in me not to become bitter.

Bitterness only corrupts, I reminded myself. *Bitterness only corrupts.*

It wasn't working. I could think only of the emotional roller coaster of the last year. We dreamed of this child, praying over the one God had for us. We spent hours hoping he or she was warm, healthy, and happy, at the same time worrying our little one was cold, sick, and afraid.

As we sped through the adoption course, we wondered which day was the child's birthday and hoped someone was making it special.

We poured every dime we owned into the process; every ounce of strength went into bringing a child home. We were about to leave Ukraine, brokenhearted and financially empty. It was over. The love we already had for a child we didn't even know seemed to be in vain. Our dream had died.

Legally, we still had one more appointment, but we knew waiting in Kiev during the Christmas and New Year's break would only waste time. The government wouldn't hand out any new appointments until the middle of January. Going home would move us to the back of the line for a new appointment, but we were running out of vacation days, and the longer we stayed the more it cost—not just financially.

Our three previously adopted children were at our home in Kansas with my aging parents. In the three weeks we had been gone, they had endured an ice storm that left them without power in a cold house for almost a week. For three days the people I loved in the United States huddled in front of a fireplace trying to keep warm, hoping the electricity would come back on.

My parents finally decided to pack up the kids and head to their home in Colorado, where it was warm and dry. Even after they were safe and comfortable, I couldn't stop worrying about them. Playing with their cousins in Colorado didn't keep them from missing us. Daily phone calls were filled with their pleas for us to come home.

The roller coaster ride we had been on in the last few days, weeks, and months was too much. We wanted off. It was time to go home.

We called our facilitator the next morning and told him he could keep looking for a child, but we were leaving December 23 whether he found a child for us or not. He had four days for a miracle. Meanwhile, we called the airlines, determined to fly out sooner. Our dream was dead. We couldn't bear to stay away from our children for nothing, especially with Christmas approaching.

My call to the airlines didn't go well. All the flights were booked. We were stuck.

Furious, I slammed down the phone and started letting my Heavenly Father have it. I yelled and screamed and berated Him for dragging us half-way around the world on a wild good chase. I was livid about the money we had spent, the emotional energy we had invested, the hearts I knew would be broken when we told our kids the news. I was furious with Him for letting me open my heart up to a child I would never know. Finally I screamed, "What do you want from us, Lord?"

Exhausted, I fell on my face before Him and cried. I don't know how long I lay there sobbing, my shoulders heaving and my breath lurching. It seemed like hours, but when I was done, I finally did what He wanted me to do all along.

"Father," I whispered with my cheek pressed against the cold tile floor, "I'm tired of this. It's all yours. Take us home or work a miracle. Whatever you want is fine." Then I fell asleep.

The next morning, seventy-two hours before we were set to fly home, we got a call. Our facilitator had found a little girl in the southern part of the country, near the Black Sea. Her health issues seemed manageable. At four years old, she was older than we had anticipated, but we would like her, he assured us. Did we want to get back on the ride?

With no time to think about it, we put our trust in our God and said yes. We were holding on for dear life, and the journey began its new leg.

Without so much as a name or a birthday to go on, we took off for Odessa to meet the little girl. We were completely in the dark about what we would find, but we weren't afraid. After all, God was in control.

Twenty-four hours later we were standing in an orphanage director's office, gazing at the most beautiful, energetic, and intriguing little girl you can imagine.

After a year of paper chasing, waiting, praying, and searching, we finally saw God's hand in the whole process. His had been with us all along, and He had finally introduced us to our little girl.

* * *

It is obvious—the Clymers were called to adopt their children. They are wonderful, loving parents, and their kids are growing up healthy and amazing. But the adoption process was not as easy as they thought it would be when they started.

As we have seen from the stories in this chapter, adoption is an amazing gift if it is God-led and God-ordained. But it is not the calling of every childless person. The most important thing is to wait on God, keep our eyes on Him, and allow Him to direct our paths.

Before you start:
- Have you exhausted the fertility treatments you are willing or able to use?
- Are both of you ready to investigate non-biological methods to start your family?
- Would you consider taking a special-needs child?
- Is your relationship with each other in a healthy state?
- Is your home in good condition and large enough for children?
- Is there anything in your background that needs to be addressed?

✻ ✻ ✻

We know that God causes all things to work together
for good to those who love God, to those who
are called according to His purpose.
—Romans 8:28

✻ ✻ ✻

Whether you decide to pursue adoption or to remain childless or you are still waiting to see what unfolds in your life, the most important thing to remember is that you are a child of God. When you give your heart to the Lord, you become a son or daughter of the King. Because of His love for you, He will use the things you go through in your life to bring what is best for you.

When we are walking through the pain of childlessness, it seems as if there will never be another joy-filled day. You are called according to God's purpose. If that call is to be an adoptive parent to a child, follow that calling. God will bless it.

Allow the wisdom God gives your spouse to guide your choices. I was ready to jump, sure that I was supposed to be an adoptive mother. John's hesitation later proved to be godly wisdom for us. It was out of worship to God that I was able to honor John's wishes and stop my quest to adopt. It does not dishonor God to pray for what you want—just stay open to the answer in case it guides you in a different direction. God may be calling you to a life that deviates from your expectations.

Lord, thank you for adopting us as your children. We know you understand our desire to be parents. Lord Jesus, we ask that you place into our home the child you have for us. Create a love in our heart for that child before we ever see his or her face. Lord, if you have called us to minister in a different way to the orphans and needy children in our world, please make that evident. Make our steps clear so that our path will follow your plan. In Jesus' name. Amen.

There is a lot of societal and familial pressure on childless couples. The thought that you would not want to adopt literally stops people in their tracks. Do not allow the expectation of outsiders to influence what God is leading you to do.

If God is calling you to adoption, by all means, do it. But if He's not calling you to the ministry of adoption—wait. Seek His wisdom, and find out what He has for you.

"Those who wait for the LORD will gain new strength; They will mount up with wings like eagles, They will run and not get tired, They will walk and not become weary" (Isaiah 40:31).

4 THE DESIRE OF OUR HEARTS

The Lord says, "I will guide you along the best pathway
for your life. I will advise you and watch over you."
—Psalm 32:8, NLT

I told John that I could accept his decision not to adopt, but I still prayed that he would change his mind. The longer I tried to convince myself that I was happy with our choice, the angrier I became. I was angry with John for being okay without children. I was angry with doctors whose names and faces I couldn't even remember because they hadn't diagnosed my PCOS when I was twenty, and I was angry with the cancer that had taken away my hope of bearing a child.

However, more than anything, I was angry with God. I didn't understand why He wanted me to suffer so much. I had been faithful, I loved the Lord with all my heart, and I wanted to be the wife and mother He had created me to be. But none of that mattered—I was going to remain childless. It felt as if I had received a death sentence.

John tried to console me. He pointed out things we did that would be inconvenient if there were children to consider. That just made it worse. I *wanted* to have a diaper bag to pack. I *wanted* to be home by 8:00 P.M. so the baby could get enough rest. I *wanted* to carry baby wipes in a purse too heavy for my shoulder. I wanted all the things that seemed like a hassle to every mother I knew.

Every time I turned on the television set, there was another news story of a child who had been hurt or abandoned by his or her parents, and my frustration grew. *How could a loving and just God allow these horrible people to have one child after the other while we so desperately wanted to be loving parents?* It just didn't make sense.

I read books on infertility, adoption, and faith. The words felt empty and false. Each story of a miracle pregnancy left me in heaving sobs.

I prayed daily for more than ten years that God would give us the child He had for us. We knew we had other options to fill our home with laughing little ones, but our own DNA would end with us.

I didn't know what to do, but I knew I couldn't go on like that. I continued to pray for a miracle child. I wanted to be like the couples whose stories I read that ended with a wonderful miracle. What made those people more worthy of parenthood than I?

No one knew the turmoil that was going on within my heart. I hid my feelings as much as I could. John knew some of what I felt, but I was careful not to badger him about it. I was smiling on the outside, telling people who asked that we had decided to be content in whatever God had for us. I was lying. I couldn't admit to the world—or to the church—that I was unwilling to trust God.

Filling our home with visiting children helped sometimes. But usually it was just a reminder of my pain. One day my great niece asked me why we didn't have any toys at our house. I didn't think much about it when I said, "Because we don't have any children living here."

She looked shocked. "No children?" she asked in her four-year-old innocence. "How do you make yourself wake up?"

She was talking about the game she liked to play every morning when she would wake her parents before they were ready to get up. But her words were painful to my ears.

I tried to find peace in reading familiar psalms. The more I searched for new revelations, the more I questioned the validity of my faith. I knew that the Bible was true, and I knew that everything Christ did on the Cross was for me, for my forgiveness and for my healing, but I felt like a spiritual failure. Not only was I physically unable to have children and emotionally unable to handle the truth, but I was also spiritually unable to trust the Creator of the universe.

I was in need of revival in my spirit. When a friend suggested I attend a retreat sponsored by a church in the neighboring town, I jumped at the chance. I wanted God to meet me in my depression and show me what I was supposed to do.

During the retreat, a woman I didn't know came to me and told me I needed to have more faith.

"If you had enough faith, you would have children," she said. Her words were stern, and I felt they were an admonishment of my spiritual immaturity. Condemnation fell hard on my heart. I explained to her that I could not have children. She looked me squarely in the face and said, "Are you limiting God's power in your life?"

"No, I know that God can do anything. That's why I'm so frustrated. I know He could give me a child if He wanted to." I was in tears.

"Child," she continued, "if you had enough faith, the God I serve would restore your uterus, and you would have a child!"

I stared at her, half in shock and half in disbelief. I couldn't believe what had just come from her mouth. I didn't doubt the creative power of God. However, suddenly I doubted the condemnation I felt when she spoke to me.

I began to laugh. I didn't mean to insult her, but this self-proclaimed prophetess could not possibly be serious! I needed to laugh, and it felt good.

My friend and I left the retreat, and on the way home we chatted about what the woman had said to me. I wasn't sure how she knew about what I was going through, but it would have been easy enough for her to find out. I mentioned it when anyone asked about children—that classic conversation-starter. One thing I was sure of was that what she said to me was not a word from the Lord.

That weekend with my friend offered respite, but the pain returned as soon as I walked through my front door. The room off the kitchen would have been perfect for a nursery, but it was still my office. The backyard would have been a wonderful place for children to play, but it was quiet—void of swings and jungle gyms that should have adorned the landscape.

When I thought I could not take another moment of empty, hollow pain, I confronted the God I wanted so desperately to trust. "I have trusted you for my family," I cried. "I know you love us, and I know you want to bless us. Why won't you?"

I sobbed and whined for hours. Frustration and anger were mingled with my pain, and the ache was so deep that I couldn't tell where it began. I was so tired of hurting.

As I lay there, curled up and feeling sorry for myself, I picked up my Bible. Thumbing through the gilded pages, I found my life's verse from the not-so-distant past, Jeremiah 29:11: "'I know the plans I have for you,' declares the LORD, 'plans to prosper you and not to harm you, plans to give you hope and a future'" (NIV).

The words struck me so funny that I laughed. *What hope? What future?* This did not feel much like prosperity to me, and I definitely did not feel protected from harm. Out of morbid curiosity I kept flipping through the pages of the book I had depended on so many times before. I landed on Psalm 37:4—"Delight yourself in the LORD and he will give you the desires of your heart."

I laughed again. "Okay, God," I said. "I have been delighting myself in you. I have served you, I have prayed to you, and I have loved you. I have trusted your love for me. Yet you have not given me the one thing I desire."

Grumbling and whining like a child, I told God what I thought. At that moment, something changed in the room. It was as if I were standing in the presence of the Holy Spirit. I sat silently, reverencing the moment. Gently, He spoke to my heart. "You have not been delighting yourself in me," He said, His voice filling my spirit. "You have been delighting yourself in the idea of being a mother."

It was truth, and it pierced the darkness in my mind. He continued lovingly. "Delight yourself in *me.* Delight yourself in the plan I have for your life, and I will place *my* desires in your heart."

Years of confusion began to make sense. "When you are seeking my best for your life, my plan will become clear to you." Peace came over me. "It is not my will for you to be sad or in anguish."

For a moment I wondered if I was imagining it, but the voice of the Father was coming through loud and clear in my heart. He was right! Becoming a mother had consumed my whole life for twelve years. In Philippians 4:11 Paul says that he learned to be content in his circumstances. It was for that reason that he could minister without longing for other things. I had not been content. My discontent sent everything spiraling out of control. God did have a plan for my life, but because I allowed myself to be needy, I became ineffective in the purpose He had for me.

Even when my life was spiraling, God had His hand on me. I needed to wait, seek His face, and listen to His voice leading my journey—

not the journey through infertility but the journey through life. Infertility was only a place of visitation that would be used by God for good.

The healing had begun. I knew that I would learn to be content in my circumstances: at peace beside the empty cradle.

* * *

John . . .

Pamela begged me to see it her way. At times, I think she really felt as if I were trying to punish her for not being able to get pregnant. I wanted to give in to her, but something I couldn't explain kept me from agreeing to adoption. Part of it was the expense, part of it was the uncertainty, but part of it was the life I had seen unfolding before us before everything was consumed by infertility and medical nightmares.

When she worked at the camp, she was so happy ministering to the girls, taking them on mission trips, and teaching them to be godly women. I knew if we had children, the ministry that was just taking flight would be grounded. I tried to talk to her about that, but she would not hear it. She argued that many women had ministries and children simultaneously.

"If God is not going to give me a child, then I don't know if I want to work in ministry." She said it out of anger, but it shocked me that she was turning her bitterness toward God.

Eventually we just stopped talking about it. I went to work and came home. She usually had supper on the table, and after we ate we sat silently watching television. It was an uncomfortable silence. After a while it was easier to stay outside working around the farm or hanging out with friends until bedtime. She didn't say much when I came in later than expected.

I never knew if I should hug her or run the other way. If I touched her, she cried; if I didn't touch her, she cried. So I stopped touching her—at least then I didn't feel as if her tears were my fault. The anger she felt about not having children caused her to overreact to everything. It was sad to watch the strong, faith-filled woman I married fly into fits of rage over the amount of time it took to brush my teeth.

I prayed for her every day, but honestly I wasn't sure if she would ever get over the dream that God would put a baby in a basket on the doorstep.

I was glad when her friend talked her into going to the retreat. She had spent so much time trying to put on a good face in public and trying to convince herself that she was supposed to be ministering to others that she was becoming spiritually bankrupt. I am quite confident that her account was severely overdrawn.

The stories she brought home from the retreat were not what I expected. I think the ridiculous nature of the woman's prophetic word was helpful, though. At least Pamela recognized it as false, so her discernment was still present. I believe that was the beginning of healing for her heart.

The day she emerged from the bedroom after spending time alone with God, I knew something was different. She was smiling. She hugged me tightly. "I am so sorry," she pressed against my chest. "You are the most amazing husband for putting up with me. I don't know God's plan for our lives, but I do know that He has one." We sat down together. "We are going to be okay without children." I could hardly believe my ears. "If God provides a child by some miracle, I won't refuse the gift. But I am finished trying to make it happen."

I was happy to have my wife back. There was still a place in her heart that had been ripped apart by the battle with infertility, but healing had begun. I knew God was about to restore her body, her mind, and her spirit for His service and to the glory of God.

❈ ❈ ❈

Many things in life seem to be insurmountable. Tragedy is around every corner. As I was learning to find peace and trust God with my life, I watched my friend Cheri go through a life-altering event that I will never have to endure.

Everyone was excited about her baby. She and her husband had tried about a year before it finally happened. The day James was born they began a new journey, but it was not the journey of parenthood they expected. Cheri and her husband, Mark, knew their journey would end in sorrow.

They were holding their beautiful baby boy, feeding him, changing him, loving him, knowing all the while that he would never sit up, never crawl, and never walk. They knew that in a few short months his muscles would surrender to a disease they didn't understand.

James was born with spinal muscular atrophy (SMA), the leading inherited cause of death in infants and toddlers. He was taken home from the hospital with hospice services in place so that his parents could care for him and love him for as long as he was with them.

Over the next four months they stayed by his side constantly. People across the country were praying, praying for healing, praying for peace, and praying that God would be with James's parents in amazing ways. His parents were praying too, longing to stop the process that was shutting his little body down before their eyes.

The funeral of an infant is one of the hardest occasions in our culture. I could not let my lifetime friend walk through this without being there for her. I arrived in California the day of the visitation.

Cheri and Mark chose to have an open casket for their baby boy. I stood with Cheri near the tiny casket, not knowing what to say. James was a beautiful baby. His thick, curly hair was like his mom's. His sweet face was angelic, even in death.

Hundreds of people came to lend their support to Cheri and Mark. They were putting on a strong front, but when I started to say goodnight, Mark asked me to stay with them until everyone else was gone. They needed my childless support in the face of hearing about everyone else's children while they were grieving their son.

I was trying to be strong for Cheri, but I couldn't hold back my tears. By the end of the evening we were both emotionally drained. From the sofa in the parlor we watched the last few visitors pass in front of James's casket, both of us crying freely.

The next morning, family and close friends gathered at the cemetery. Cheri could not watch as they lowered James's little blue casket into the earth. Mark ushered her gently to the graveside where her family tradition dictated that she place the first dirt in the grave.

She collapsed. Digging her slim fingers hard into the loose soil, she moaned in agony as she pushed a handful past the crumbling edge. Mark helped her to her feet and held her as they watched the mourners return to their normal lives. For Cheri and Mark, it didn't feel as if life would ever be normal again.

Because SMA is a genetically transferred condition, Mark and Cheri were afraid to try again—at least until they endured the genetic profiling to determine the likelihood of their next child being born with the abnormality. They found out that SMA is inherited only when both parents carry the defective gene, shattering their hope of having a family. They weren't willing to risk the life of another child.

Watching our friends lose their baby after holding him and caring for him showed me a side of grace I had not imagined in being childless. I will never feel the pain associated with burying my child. There is never going to be a knock on my door telling me my child has been in an accident, and I won't wait up at night hoping to hear teenagers sneak into their rooms twenty minutes past curfew.

Being there for Cheri and Mark affirmed for me the way God uses us, not only in spite of our pain but sometimes also *because* of our pain. I thought I was the last person who could comfort them. But to Cheri and Mark, I was the one who could give them my time without constraint.

Becoming content with a childless life looks different for everyone. Not everyone is called to ministry or a lofty career; nevertheless, each of us has a calling. We are all called to love. If that love cannot be given to a child, God will use it in other ways. The secret is to remain open to His direction and willing to say yes to His call.

Walking closely with the Lord is the only thing that can bring contentment in any situation that is out of line with our deepest desires and dreams. Allowing the joy of the Lord to flow through our lives doesn't discount what we've been through. On the contrary, it reinforces the strength of our witness when we are joyful in the face of disappointment.

Contentment is sometimes a choice one makes when things aren't necessarily going well. There are also times when contentment comes easily. When it doesn't come easily, it is important to accept that there are things in life we can't change. The Serenity Prayer, often associated with addiction recovery, also promotes peace in other life-disrupting situations.

> *God, grant me the serenity to accept the things I cannot change; the courage to change the things I can; and the wisdom to know the difference.*

Vicki Sprouse shares her story of finding peace during trying times:

> When I was in my thirties and well into my journey with infertility, I looked at my future in this way: *By age forty I will have a child. If not, I will have moved on with my life.* It turns out that isn't the way it happened.

Now, as I approach forty-two, I still don't have a child, and I still haven't moved on with my life, and I'm often depressed about it. It doesn't matter how many times I put on a brave face and will myself to get over it and move on—I am constantly pulled back to my discontent by outside forces, especially the ones I love who are deeply affected by my inability to produce offspring.

It's one thing to experience personal disappointment that is mine alone, but it's another to have disappointment that sends a thermonuclear shockwave throughout my family.

Every visit, vacation, and holiday with the family becomes a torturous exercise in walking on eggshells, knowing that someone is going to notice. There is nowhere to hide it, and no way to avoid it. Our children simply are not there.

Christmas and birthday parties are torturous reminders that we have no one of our own to watch open gifts and experience new joys. I watch my husband's face and sense his emotional withdrawal when his niece and nephews open their presents. My mom, the non-grandmother-not-by-choice, fights back tears as her peers pull out pictures of their grandchildren or announce a new grandchild on the way.

Of course, they don't blame me, and they love me too much to say anything. There are subtle but glaring reminders that say it. My inability to have children has deeply affected everyone in my family.

There are times when a family member's grief is so apparent that I feel as if I'm in an emotional concentration camp because of something over which I have absolutely no control. When that happens, I feel like running away.

I struggle to make it through family events. I love my family, but I've come to the place at which I cannot face another visit. Childlessness covers me in darkness.

I experienced a particularly difficult time when I flew into a fit of anger, spewing my emotional poison everywhere. The burden of infertility had completely enveloped my spirit, and for two days I didn't care if I lived or died. I was unable to work and had to self-medicate just to sleep. It took everything I had just to hold my head upright and put one foot in front of the other. I was broken.

Finally, the fear of a possible hospitalization pulled me out of myself long enough to think rationally. I was not going to let an eighteen-year-long barren-womb prison sentence steal my freedom. I knew I had to do something to free myself from the captivity of my circumstances.

Pulling out of that break, I came to the inner realization of the damage eighteen years of walking the path of infertility can do. It is devastating and emotionally and spiritually crippling. My personality had changed so drastically that my husband didn't know me and no longer knew how to react to me. I was so angry with God that my faith began to ring hollow.

I meet women who are walking this path of childlessness who seem to have it all together. Deep down I wonder if they really do or if they have just practiced looking happy. How do they go on with their lives so easily when eighteen years later I feel as if I'm constantly starting back at square one?

Making peace with your circumstances does not mean that you must pretend you never wanted children. Peace doesn't mean that you must deny the grief you feel. In fact, it *allows* you to grieve.

It is often difficult for people on the outside to realize the very real loss childless couples endure. There are several degrees of loss in the process, and coping with each loss during the process individually— from difficulty getting pregnant to permanent infertility to accepting childlessness—is exhausting. By the time a couple has processed each loss and moved past it, the next is rearing its head.

When my mother-in-law was in her last stages with cancer, I cared for her in her home. As we tried to prepare our hearts to say good-bye to her, the hospice chaplain gave us a booklet setting out the Kübler-Ross model of the five stages of grief most people experience. As I read the list he gave us, I realized it was the same process John and I experienced from childlessness.

The first stage is *denial and isolation.* It's the stage when we say, "I feel fine," or "This can't be happening to me."

When considering the death of a loved one, the dissolution of a marriage, or the loss of a job, it is easy to understand how unhealthy denial is. Those are permanent, unchangeable losses. People grieve the loss, but they know there is nothing they can do to change it.

Denial is a long, complicated stage when dealing with infertility. Until tests and experience prove otherwise, there is still hope. Hope prevents us from accepting the end of a dream. Hope compels us never to give up. We deny that the infertility is permanent and pray that, if it is, God will send a miracle either to cure us or to allow us to bring a child into our family through another method.

Even after I knew we would not adopt, I denied it by praying that God would put a baby in our lives through a miracle that John could not argue with. I couldn't even pass a cardboard box on the highway without stopping to make sure someone hadn't left a child in it. I had seen a news story about such an incident when I was a teenager and actually wondered if it might happen again to bring me the child God had for me. I was in deep denial that our childlessness was permanent.

When in denial, it is painful to watch others capturing the dream we can't let go of. Isolation becomes comfortable, even for those who normally surround themselves with people. It is easier to stay home than it is to deal with babies everywhere. Surrounded by solitude, we don't have to face our loss. We suffer anyway though, gripped by longing and filled with grief.

I didn't realize how much I was isolating myself until I received a card in the mail from my friend Ginney.

> I miss you, girlfriend. You must be really busy, but we need to go to lunch soon. I need you, my friend. And you need me too. Call me! Love, Ginney.

Her note was short, but it was just what I needed to push me out of my emotional cocoon. She reminded me that I was not an island. Lunch with her a few days later proved to be the release I needed to realize that I needed my friends—even when I couldn't be the strong one.

Once denial subsides and we come to terms with the fact that the loss is permanent, *anger* steps in.

For me, anger came in many forms. When it was least expected, I flew into fits of tears or rage. I tried to keep a cap on my anger, because I thought it was the right thing to do. I wanted everyone to see that I was fine, but I was not fine. Even though it was not my fault that I couldn't have a child, I was angrier with myself than anyone or anything else.

In the anger phase of grief it is important to find someone to talk with. A counseling pastor, Christian therapist, or biblical counselor can help tremendously during this stage of grief. Don't be afraid to share your heart with a trusted friend or relative. God puts people in our lives for times like this. He knows our grief even better than we do, and He cares about every need. Take advantage of the blessing of friendships He provides.

Try not to take your anger out on your spouse. Remember—he is grieving too. Just because he isn't responding to grief in a way you understand does not discount his pain of childlessness. Even the most rational man grieves the loss of the children he wanted to love.

Take a deep breath—that always helps. But once anger wanes, the need to find another way may grow stronger.

Bargaining, no matter how irrational, is typically the next step in the grieving process.

I bargained with John to change his mind about adoption. I bargained in my own mind, trying to find the emotional currency to be smart enough to fix our infertility. But mostly I bargained with God. I spent my prayer time begging for a child, willing to give up anything else in my life. *Lord, if I could just become pregnant I will be a better wife.* Or *Dear God, I promise to raise my child to be a missionary if you would just put a baby in our lives.*

I would have given anything for a child, even when I knew there was nothing I could offer that would change anything.

Finding out the desire to fix it is a normal part of grief gave me the freedom to stop trying to bargain. The chips were simply not mine to trade.

When anger and bargaining have done nothing to fix the situation, *depression* sets in. If allowed to linger and take root, depression can be the most dangerous of the five stages of grief. Childless couples are especially prone to depression. The lack of validation from the parenting world allows mild cases of depression to become apathy. For some, apathy is the drug of choice to numb their pain.

When depression and apathy hit as a result of grief, there are three choices: to be charmed by it, to be harmed by it, or to be alarmed by it.

Depression may initially feel like relief. It isn't until the depression becomes rooted in the mind and spirit that the damage it brings becomes evident. In the stillness of its wake is a deep pit wooing us with the supposed peace found in the depth. In the false sense of peace it provides we may not notice the darkness of lost hope that causes the hardness of heart that presses inward while pushing others away.

People locked in depression may look fine on the outside, but they have often disconnected emotionally and are functioning on auto-pilot much of the time. They may grow spiritually distant from the Lord and avoid interaction with their spouses or other family members.

After allowing depression to take residency in our lives, we may find that even simple activities become laborious. Getting out of bed, taking a shower, and eating may be delayed or avoided altogether. A shroud of despair clouds every thought, and even a kind word from a stranger may bring a flood of tears. This is when depression becomes harmful. If you or your spouse are facing any stage of depression over infertility and childlessness—or any other life situation—I strongly recommend counseling with a certified biblical counselor. Many churches offer this service free of charge. It is important to speak to a professional and to allow him or her to guide you to medical care if necessary.

The good news is that depression brought by grief can be overcome. God's Word promises that we will not face trials alone. 1 Corinthians 10:13 says, "No temptation has overtaken you but such as is common to man; and God is faithful, who will not allow you to be tempted beyond what you are able, but with the temptation will provide the way of escape also, so that you will be able to endure it."

One of the first steps away from depression is to change your focus. When my focus was completely directed at my determination to have a child one way or another, I couldn't see anything else clearly. I couldn't look at what God had for my life without children, and depression took over. It wasn't until I stared into the heart of God that things changed.

Try smashing an insect with a fly-swatter without looking. You will miss. Focusing on Christ and spending time in God's Word puts us in a healthier mind-set, thus giving us the ability to deal with the darkness brought by depression.

Focusing on Christ in the midst of depression is not easy, and I am not trying to make it sound too simple. You may have to take baby steps out of the emotional swamp. As you begin to focus on God's Word and the blessings in your life, those steps will get bigger, and eventually you will find true peace in the Lord rather than the temporal charm of emotional black holes.

Finally, we come to the stage of grief that allows us to move forward: *acceptance.* Acceptance does not mean that you will feel ready to *embrace* a childless life but that you will be able to move forward with life. Not trying to fix things that are out of your control, not feeling angry, and not remaining stuck in a black cloud—but putting one foot in front of the other will lead you toward the full life God has for you.

The decision to make peace with your circumstances doesn't always follow a divine revelation. Coming to the end of the journey with infertility and simply saying, "Enough!" can bring you to a place of contentment with what the Lord has provided.

Joanne Fitzgerald came to peace and contentment after years in the trenches and several miscarriages:

> Growing up the youngest of three daughters in a military family, I always pictured my adult life living in an old, white farmhouse with a wraparound porch. I imagined a screen door slamming as children ran in and out all day long. After growing up in a silent house, I wanted a household full of laughter and joy.
>
> I enjoyed my college years, selecting a major by default. I did not truly see myself in a career; I wanted to be a wife and mother and stay at home with my children and make a home for my husband. I met a man my junior year in college whose plan for his future fit my ideal, including children.
>
> I followed him and his plan. We spent the early years of our marriage working to pay bills and put off starting a family until we felt we were ready. Several years into our marriage, I received a diagnosis of endometriosis. The doctor told us that because of this diagnosis, the best time for us to try to have a family was upon us. We didn't even consider his suggestion.
>
> I told myself that I did not want my body to plan our lives, so we waited another year. When we decided we were ready to try for that family, we were able to get pregnant very quickly, but we lost the baby at six weeks. My husband was engrossed in work and elected not to come home to be with me as I went through the mis-

carriage. I had not told my parents because their first grandchild was due any day, and I did not want to take away from her birth. I was alone with my anguish.

Another year went by. I went through treatments for the endometriosis, and we began fertility testing. Doctors discovered issues with mobility, quality, and compatibility. We overheard a technician say aloud, "His sperm are getting killed."

My husband looked at me in disgust. As the months went by, he started calling me the "baby killer." His physical and emotional abuse continued, but I refused to admit our marriage was not the fairy tale of my dreams. I told no one of the abuse, and I stayed in the marriage.

We decided to save for in vitro fertilization. All I knew was that I wanted to be a mother, and my whole focus was on that goal.

One day I had a vision. I saw myself holding the hands of two beautiful blonde girls, one about six and one four, my daughters. They were laughing and walking with me. Then I saw my face. I was gone—my eyes empty, without a soul, with only my body left to take care of those beautiful girls. I knew without a doubt that if I stayed in that marriage, my soul and self would be gone.

In my selfishness, I was willing to bring children into this abusive marriage. It scared me so much that I told my husband that I no longer wanted to do in vitro. I never mentioned my vision. My desire for children had overshadowed everything else in my life. God clearly showed me that my desire was not right.

I left my abusive marriage with only $100 and my clothes in trash bags. As I headed out the door, my husband tried to stop me, wielding a gun in my face as I stood in the doorway. I kept walking. I promised myself that I would always live honestly, true to my heart's desire.

I did not mourn my marriage, but I mourned the dream of a child put on hold by the abuse.

It took years for healing and restoration to be complete in my heart. I met a man who had two daughters from a previous marriage. As we discussed entering a serious relationship, I told him not to be with me if he didn't want another child. Not having a child of my own was a deal-breaker in my heart. He was fifteen years older than me, but he told me he did indeed want to have a child with me. Eventually we married. I could think of nothing but starting my family with my wonderful new husband.

After a heart scare, he shared with me that he could not give me my dream. As the oldest son of an Irish family, he had been working since he was a young boy. Now, with his daughters in college, he just could not start over again. He truly wanted to give me a child, but he just could not. I understood.

He offered to release me from our marriage, but I refused even to think of that option. I had the joyful household I dreamed of as a child, and my heart was full. I needed to let go of my dream to be a mother.

The doctor told us that I, at the age of forty-two, had only a zero-to-one-percent chance of getting pregnant. We relaxed and began to enjoy our marriage without the pressure to conceive or the necessity to prevent it.

After a vacation, we found ourselves with a surprise. I took three pregnancy tests that were positive and considered it a miracle pregnancy. I was already envisioning our daughter's baptism and first day of school. The years rolled out in front of me. Although we hadn't planned this pregnancy, joy filled my heart. My husband was by my side, supporting my dream and my elation.

When that pregnancy ended in miscarriage, I was devastated. We had seen the sac with the embryo. This was our baby, and we had to say goodbye.

After the dilation and curretage (DNC) we went home together in our sorrow. I was numb. I wanted to hold her, to feel her life. I wanted to stay in the dream. I saw her on the ultrasound. I mourned her. In my memory box, just for her, I placed the ultrasound photos, three pregnancy tests, and her name, Elizabeth Grace—the only proof I had that she ever existed.

I asked my husband if we could try again. He said no and offered again to release me from our marriage. I told him I was not leaving. I knew God had sent him into my life, but I just couldn't believe my heart's desire to be a mother was not to be. Clearly, it was not.

I have struggled as I mourn these lost children of mine. I have struggled to find joy in my life. Now, five years after the last miscarriage, I have learned a few things. I have learned to rejoice in what God has given me: a wonderful husband, two stepdaughters, a loving dog that sits with me when I cry, and a household of joy.

I think I will always feel the sorrow of not meeting Elizabeth Grace. I still know the disappointment of not seeing her blue eyes or knowing if she would have been blonde like me or carried the Irish red hair of her father. Yet I know that my life has been God-guided and God-directed. He has cried with me in my mourning, held me when I felt as if I were the only one missing my child, and rejoiced in my marriage. He walks with me.

My desire is to be God's child, to honor Him in a way that is good. I feel my legacy will be that I have loved well. That will be enough.

You are not to blame for your infertility.

You are not responsible for the pain others feel.

You cannot carry grief for someone else.

No one else can carry your grief.

Jesus said that we should cast our cares upon Him. Then take His yoke upon us, for His burden is light.

Establish emotional boundaries to safeguard your heart during holidays and family events.

Ask the Lord to show you His plan for your life

Your identity is not that of a barren woman.

Who does Christ say that you are?

Vicki told me that her experience with the grief made her feel like Forrest Gump:

I think of the scene in *Forrest Gump* when his grief gets the best of him. He just takes off running with no particular destination.

He said, "I just ran." I understand why Forrest "just ran." He needed to get away from the noise of his grief and concentrate on something else for a while. I have to find my equivalent of the 3,000-mile Forrest Gump marathon and discover something else to concentrate on besides my loss.

I don't know what that will be. It may be something as simple as changing my daily routine and my thought patterns, or maybe something as big as going to school, making a change, or moving to a new location. My husband is on this journey with me, so I have to be sensitive to his needs and desires along the way. Maybe we'll just run together.

Eventually Forrest Gump stopped running. The day that happened, he said, "I'm pretty tired—I think I'll go home now."

The journey through the steps of grief caused by childlessness is tiring. The desire to run can be consuming, but the result is emotional and physical exhaustion. It's time to come home. Unlike Forrest Gump, you have a loving Father waiting for you with arms outstretched. Stop running, and let Him love you through the grief.

"Create in me a clean heart, O God, And renew a steadfast spirit within me. Do not cast me away from Your presence And do not take Your Holy Spirit from me. Restore to me the joy of Your salvation And sustain me with a willing spirit" *(Psalm 51:10-12).*

The battle through infertility may leave you feeling spent. Spiritual and emotional bankruptcy is dangerous. It leaves its victims lacking joy and without strength to carry on. None of that is from the Lord, but that does not mean that believers are immune to the effects.

David understood what it was like to lack spiritual zeal. Many times in the Psalms he asks for restoration. Psalm 51:10-12 spoke to my heart often. I came back time and time again to sit with my Heavenly Father and meditate on His Word.

My heart had become hard, and the thoughts I allowed to dwell there had left deep scars, but God made it clean. He alone had the power to renew my spirit and pull it from despair.

My anger caused me to fear that I was no longer worthy of being called a child of God. The truth is that none of us is ever worthy. The Bible says that we are called the sons and daughters of God. That adoption is a gift afforded by the grace God bestows on us when we step out in faith. Our faith in Christ is what allows the Holy Spirit to be present in our life. It is not God pulling himself from us, but our refusing to walk with Him. When I read the last line in verse twelve, everything made sense. I needed to submit my spirit to God so that He could make me willing. A willing vessel can be used, even if it is broken. It is unyielding clay that will never find contentment.

God knows the tears we cry, the fears we hold, and the faith we have lost. When life becomes too painful and we think we cannot go on, remember that the Lord is *El Roi,* the God who sees me. He promises plans and purposes for our lives beyond what we can see. We must trust in His wisdom and omniscience.

In Christ there is restoration, there is healing, and there is peace. He will walk with you as you learn to find peace and contentment in your circumstances. He is bigger than whatever plagues you. Believers are not called to be trapped under our circumstances but to be raised victoriously through Christ, who gives us strength to face everything that life hands us.

When we trust Him fully, without exception, He will lead us to the contentment we crave.

Dear Lord, I need you to meet me where I am today. Search my heart. You know my struggles. You know the things that have broken me and bound me in confusion. God, I pray that you would take those things from me. Father, I want to have a renewed spirit. I need the joy of your salvation in my life. Help me find the contentment that comes only from you. I want to follow you throughout my life. Let your ways become my ways, your thoughts become my thoughts, and your desires for my life become my desires. I give it all to you, Lord. In Jesus' name I pray. Amen.

5 PROTECTING YOUR MARRIAGE

Everyone who hears these words of Mine and acts on them, may be compared to a wise man who built his house on the rock. And the rain fell, and the floods came, and the winds blew and slammed against that house; and yet it did not fall, for it had been founded on the rock.

—Matthew 7:24-25

Little data is available that cites the direct effect of childlessness or infertility on divorce rates. However, the inability to have a family has been known to cause divisions in marriages. Ignored, such a division can eventually lead to divorce. It is important to protect your marriage during your battle with infertility and childlessness.[1]

When we decided to have children, we knew our relationship was established on a solid foundation in Christ. We loved the Lord and were active in our church. John was on the board of directors at our church, led Royal Rangers, and worked with me in the children's ministry program on Sunday evenings.

Parenting can be hard on a marriage, so we took steps to make sure we were on the same page about discipline, dietary choices, and schools. We discussed worst-case-scenarios, like our baby having a birth defect. What if he or she had special needs in school? We thought we had covered every possible situation that would require us to be in agreement and make quick decisions. We never talked about what we would do to stay like-minded if we didn't have children.

The internal conflicts John and I went through during our struggle with infertility left us with a lot of unanswered questions and frustrations that we never addressed. There were so many things we said to each other that couldn't be taken back. Things we thought but didn't say caused bitterness in our hearts.

When I finally reached the point of acceptance with our childlessness, I thought we would be okay. It wasn't that simple. Many important things from the early years of our marriage became casualties during our years of battle. We wanted to love one another, and we wanted to be happily married for the rest of our lives. We just didn't know how.

We had seen God's hand in our lives before. He was always with us, even in our childlessness, and it was good. Romans 8:28 says, "We know that God causes all things to work together for good to those who love God, to those who are called according to His purpose."

God faithfully brought John and me through marriage-threatening situations in the past. There was no reason to think He wouldn't do it again.

Still, we were not prepared for the effect permanent childlessness had on our marriage. This journey brought us into the darkest emotional valleys either of us had ever experienced. It forced us to rethink our dreams, change our plans, and question our faith.

Making peace with a life without children was only part of the healing process. We had accepted the finality of our life circumstance, and we were learning to lean on the Lord to place His desires for our lives in our hearts. Unfortunately, in the years before we arrived at that place, we allowed a stronghold in our home. Apathy had fumigated our home with its poison. We didn't remember how to love one another, and we weren't sure it mattered anymore. Our life together was reduced to coexistence out of obligation.

Anguish subsided with our desire to follow God's leading as closely as we could. However, the space between us was growing wider. Inertia from the rift was dividing our home.

We knew that if we did nothing, a household God had created was going to fall. We were focused on the sands of infertility, medical problems, and disappointment so much that it blurred our view of the

Rock that was the foundation of our relationship. We had to fix our eyes on Jesus and put our marriage into His hands.

Forgiveness Is Key

To bridge the wide expanse growing between our hearts, it was necessary for us to forgive one another for the disappointment we felt. I didn't blame John, and he said he didn't blame me, for our childless plight. But as we walked on eggshells and avoided each other, it became obvious that we were indeed holding offense in our hearts.

As I searched scriptures about forgiveness, I found that there is no biblical basis for thinking of forgiveness as a process. Forgiveness is obedience to God. We choose each day, at every potential offense, whether or not we will forgive.

Our choice to forgive is a direct reflection of the relationship God has with us. He chose to give us a way to be in right relationship with Him through the forgiveness offered by the Cross. We are forgiven; therefore, we too must forgive. Colossians 3:12-13 says, "As those who have been chosen of God, holy and beloved, put on a heart of compassion, kindness, humility, gentleness and patience; bearing with one another, and forgiving each other, whoever has a complaint against anyone; just as the Lord forgave you, so also should you."

Forgiveness is required if our relationship with God is going to be intact. If that relationship is out of sync, our marriage cannot possibly be on a solid foundation of faith.

Divorce Is Not an Option

At times we became so frustrated with each other that we just wanted out. When apathy was at its highest level in our home, we thought about separating. Our reasoning was that we were still young enough to find new spouses who would be better fit for our family goals. John could find a wife who could bear children, and I could find a husband who would want to adopt.

As soon as the thought became words, we both knew it was wrong. But there it was, like the elephant in the room. Words can be like acid, and the damage they invoke cannot be taken back. Couples must choose their words carefully and prayerfully, especially during times of struggle.

It was around Christmastime, and I was reading "The Gift of the Magi" by O. Henry. As the story goes, Phil Dillingham sells his prized pocket watch to purchase jeweled, tortoise shell combs for his wife's beautiful long hair. At the same time, she cut her hair and sold it to a wigmaker in order to afford a chain for his watch. The story is intended to show sacrificial love.

As I read it that year, I realized that we were doing the same thing as the couple in the story. We were considering giving up our marriage, the most important relationship in either of our lives, to allow the other a chance at children, a chance that was based on speculation and unfounded possibilities. Nothing about the idea was based upon what we valued together. Nothing about a divorce was in line with God's plan for our lives. We had no idea how we had reached the point that we were willing to sacrifice the vow we had made to each other and to God. How could we think we had the right to divide what God had brought together for a purpose, even if we didn't see the purpose at the time?

The thought of spending the rest of our lives apart and breaking our vow to God was shocking. Our hearts changed toward each other. For the first time in more than five years, we could see each other as the one God brought to us.

The ridiculousness of the thought of separating because our life together was different than what we envisioned was alarming. Not only did we need to spend more time together, but we also needed to spend a lot more time seeking the Lord for our marriage.

John still didn't want to adopt, and I was still struggling to accept childlessness as permanent, but our marriage was not up for grabs. It was time to rebuild what infertility had attempted to steal.

The first step in reclaiming our home was for me to give my burden and desires to the Lord. If we truly believe that Jesus died and rose again to bear our sorrow and pain as well as our sin, we must be willing to lay it all down before Him.

When people face trials, it is often difficult to remember to make marriage a priority. For a moment, try to imagine life without your spouse. If this is the person you want to have children with, raise your family with, and grow old with, it probably makes you extremely sad to think of life without him. In most relationships, picturing your life without your spouse is enough to make you feel grateful for the life you have with him, with or without the children you desire.

> This is another thing you do: you cover the altar of the LORD with tears, with weeping and with groaning, because He no longer regards the offering or accepts it with favor from your hand. Yet you say, "For what reason?" Because the LORD has been a witness between you and the wife of your youth, against whom you have dealt treacherously, though she is your companion and your wife by covenant. But not one has done so who has a remnant of the Spirit. And what did that one do while he was seeking a godly off-spring? Take heed then to your spirit, and let no one deal treacherously against the wife of your youth. "For I hate divorce," says the LORD, the God of Israel, "and him who covers his garment with wrong," says the LORD of hosts. "So take heed to your spirit, that you do not deal treacherously" *(Malachi 2:13-16).*

It is clear that childlessness is not a reason for divorce. In fact, there is no reason to petition for a divorce outside of adultery or marital abandonment by an unbelieving spouse.

God knows that marriage is not the easiest road. Paul said in 1 Corinthians 7:28, "If you marry, you have not sinned; and if a virgin marries, she has not sinned. Yet such will have trouble in this life, and I am trying to spare you."

God never promised that we would not have pain in our lives. That's why He took that pain upon himself. He knew we could not bear it alone. Isaiah 53:4 says, "Surely our griefs He Himself bore, And our sorrows He carried; Yet we ourselves esteemed Him stricken, Smitten of God, and afflicted."

Knowing that God hates divorce and that He understands what we are going through is crucial in protecting a marriage during life's storms. He knows they will come, and He knows how to lead us through them.

The Personality Factor

We must allow our spouse to react to infertility and childlessness according to the personality God gave him. Without understanding why we react the way we do, both partners may end up feeling misunderstood and frustrated; adding to the stressors already present due to infertility.

There are four basic personality types. Understanding the personalities helps with communication and with meeting the emotional needs of each other. Taking the time to discover the God-given personality of those to whom we are close can help us treat each other with more respect and appreciation.

Those with the *popular sanguine* personality are fun-loving and creative. They need your attention, affection, and approval. They will fill their lives with things to make them happy. Going through infertility and childlessness, they will hold onto hope for as long as there is even a slim chance that something will change. The sanguine is the silver lining on a cloudy day. If you are married to a sanguine, he will cheer you up and cheer you on. The popular sanguine trusts easily and shares openly. This type of person is deeply hurt if he feels rejected. But the popular sanguine forgives quickly and hopes that others will forgive his or her mistakes as well.

The *powerful choleric* is a take-charge person. He or she wants results quickly and needs to be in control of life. Choleric people admire loyalty and need to know others appreciate them. They make great leaders and often have careers that encourage their leadership skills. The powerful choleric has a need to correct wrongs and will push to find answers. This person is not easily discouraged, but if it's impossible to win, he or she will walk away from the situation. Powerful choleric spouses can seem unemotional and detached. It is their stoic demeanor that allows them to keep a clear head when others are being ruled by emotional tides.

The deep and thoughtful *perfect melancholy* is well organized and analytical and has usually considered every option before the physician completes the diagnostic tests. People with this personality have planned their lives from childhood and are not easily diverted from the plan. Melancholies will find every piece of information related to the infertility diagnosis and research treatments and potential cures. When they realize their plans are not going to happen, they may withdraw into depression.

The most low-key personality is the *peaceful phlegmatic.* Easygoing and relaxed, the kind-hearted phlegmatic takes life as it comes.

This person keeps his or her emotions hidden most of the time, and it may be hard to tell how affected such a person is to his or her child-less state. Peaceful phlegmatic people handle pressure and stress well. They may opt out of complicated medical procedures if the results are not guaranteed. Phlegmatics are likely to choose the simple pleasures in life. They avoid turmoil and conflict as much as possible.[2]

Understanding that John's personality is a combination of melan-choly and choleric helped me realize why he reacted to events in our life so much differently than I. He needed to shut down emotionally so that he could maintain his strength. He needed to be alone sometimes. He had to keep himself busy with work, because that was something he could control. His distance under pressure is not a reflection of his love for me. It is the inborn defense mechanism that makes him func-tion in the face of pain.

I am a combination of popular sanguine and powerful choleric. I needed to talk about our plight. I needed to be validated as still being lovable, and I needed to find a solution that would give me the out-come I wanted. The tougher things are around me, the more I talk and the more I try to fix them. It is difficult but necessary to understand that not everything should be fixed.

Personalities are a huge factor in the way we deal with things, but they are not an excuse to treat each other badly. In fact, the knowledge of the personality types should be used only as a point of understand-ing and communication, not as a weapon to justify anger toward your spouse for the way he reacted to the pain in life.

There were times when John thought he had to be strong because I was falling apart. He was trying to be the support beam so that I wouldn't crumble. But all I saw was a hard heart. By the same token, when I tried to draw him out and begged him to talk about his feel-ings, thinking it would help, he saw it as nagging. We were both at-tempting to give the other what we actually needed ourselves.

Communication was seized by self-interest and pride, disguised as concern for one another. We were so lost in our own emotions that we didn't realize we had not asked the other person what he or she needed. Our well-intended gestures tore at our marriage, fraying the seams of a relationship we would have called rock solid.

When I began to understand the personalities, I experienced many "ah-ha" moments. I was able to appreciate John's quiet strength and react to him in ways that supported his strengths rather than provoked his weaknesses.

Communication Trumps Assumption

The battle with infertility is one of the most painful experiences a couple can endure. Keep in mind as you weather those marital storms that we are warned in 1 Corinthians 7:27-28 that those who marry will face many troubles in this life.

Many couples struggle because one partner wants to talk about feelings while the other thinks there's nothing to talk about. It is not unusual for a man to be emotionally distant. He may really feel that there is nothing to talk about, but he may be embarrassed or even ashamed if he is dealing with male infertility. For a man, the thought of being unable to father a child goes beyond the desire to parent and reaches into his feelings of masculinity and security. Admitting his fears and concerns can make him feel weak in a time when he needs to be in control.

Dealing with the emotional disconnect in marriage is not always easy, but it is imperative if your marriage is going to survive childlessness or any other decision that requires compromise by one or both partners.

If couples can remind themselves that their common desire to have a child does not mean that their emotional responses will be the same, it is possible to walk through this journey with understanding and come through it closer than ever before. Keeping your marriage as your first priority is difficult, but it is necessary in a relationship that honors God.

Too often couples believe that because they are going through the same situation, they know one another's feelings. Vikki Sprouse found it difficult to deal with her husband when she thought he was handling their infertility without being emotionally affected as much as she was. She learned that she was wrong when her husband fell apart.

Don't assume your spouse is okay just because you don't see his emotions. During my infertility treatments, my husband seemed detached. At one point, he told me he had faith that we would have kids but that he was merely supporting me during the treatments because he knew I needed to feel as if I could do something about it. He didn't think the treatments were the answer to having children.

Through failure after failure he never cried; he never mourned. He told me to pull myself together and didn't want me to express my pain. It made me angry. He seemed so insensitive to my feelings. I often wondered if he really wanted kids.

Eventually I moved beyond the anger. I have come to understand that we are two people who feel differently and at different emotional degrees. It took a long time to understand that it is actually okay.

Three years after our last failed attempt, he called me from school. His voice was shaking as he reported that he left early in hysterical tears. I had never seen him cry. In fact, I happen to know that he had never cried as an adult, not even when his beloved grandfather died. But there he was, in tears, nearly inconsolable.

My indifferent husband could not maintain his facade of strength for another day. He was sad, he was angry at God for putting us through childlessness, and he was desperate for children. For the first time, he allowed himself to think about the fact that it might never happen.

His mask began to crumble on Thanksgiving. As the family gathered in the living room, his niece and nephew took center stage. Everyone was delighted with their cute toddler antics. We sat watching, wishing, wanting our children to be there too, wondering when a family gathering wouldn't be a painful reminder of our infertility.

The day his world fell apart the catalyst was a lecture at school. As a student, he had been in attendance during every topic known to education. But this time was different. As the guest speaker told the audience about the female reproductive system, my strong husband fell apart.

For years I had assumed he was calloused and uncaring about our infertility and about my feelings. I had questioned his peace in this situation and wondered how he could be so disconnected from my pain.

The day he broke down was bittersweet. I was thrilled that he was finally feeling something like what I was feeling. I felt connected to him, and I was so happy to know that he understood. For the first time in years, he wasn't shoving his feelings deeper than he could let me see.

On the other hand, I was frightened. I had learned to deal with my pain myself. But I didn't know how to help him. I was afraid he might not be able to stop the emotional response that brought him to these tears.

A few days later, the bill for cryopreservation came. My husband was home and intercepted the mail. We know when to expect it. It comes every year—the rent for our embryos that will likely never be our children. I usually just tell him it came and to pay the bill. When he went back to school, we decided to stop trying. We rationalized that we should take one step at a time. That's why it shocked me that he hid it from me when he saw it. He said he wanted to enjoy the weekend without thinking about what might or might not be. We spent those days hunting for the perfect Christmas tree. We sipped cider at a little coffee shop and just enjoyed being together. I didn't know until Monday morning that the bill had come. My husband was protecting me, and I felt safe with him for the first time in three years.

Don't wait for your husband to have a breakdown before you trust his love for you and his desire to share your goals for children. In treating your spouse with respect and compassion, you give him permission to share his heart freely with you.

Talk about what each of you needs. That is often easier said than done, and it is helpful for some couples to see a biblical counselor who has experience with couples coping with childlessness.

Change Perspective

After years of trying to conceive, our marriage became identified with infertility, cancer, and defectiveness. Even with contentment and God's peace, we were the marriage without children. We didn't fit with other couples our age, because they had children. We didn't fit with younger couples, because they were hopeful about future children. Older adults had grandchildren. Everywhere we looked, reflections of a barren womb stared back at us.

When the perspective by which you look at your life is causing strife, it is necessary to change that perspective. When God led us to contentment without children, He had a plan for our lives. We prayed for Him to give us a clear vision of what we were to do next. Still, though, we labeled our relationship.

There is power in our words, and the enemy will use them against us. When we called our marriage "infertile," "defective," and "damaged," it became just that. We thought God would still use us *in spite* of our childlessness, still discounting the validity of our family unit.

Embracing the home and family that God assigned to us took time. Changing our personal label from "childless couple" to "family of two" acknowledged that our home was valid and that God valued us as a family. Speaking positives into our household brought a different attitude to our home. We were no longer "that couple who can't have kids." We were the Sonnenmosers, the couple for whom God has amazing plans.

When we begin to see what God sees when He looks into our home, we will find freedom in the calling He has placed there. From God's vantage point we were not defective and undesirable. His view showed His children under His wing, being perfected by faith and placing their lives in His hands.

Vent Without Venom

Beyond the obvious stress of coming to terms with a childless life, the path through infertility and wrestling with whether or not to adopt creates physical, emotional, and financial pressure. Couples must protect their marriages during the whole process. Rather than waiting until anger or apathy takes over, safeguard your marriage with strategic goals that will keep you on the same page.

Keep a journal of your emotions, thoughts, dreams, and frustrations. If you have never kept a journal before, this is a great time to start. Don't worry about being eloquent—just be honest. You can write anything you think or feel. It will help you communicate more clearly with your spouse if you have already expressed your feelings.

I began journaling before I went to the doctor for our first infertility consultation. John is not interested in discussing every emotion and detail. I am. So to avoid getting on his nerves, I decided to journal the process. At the time, my intent was to have a book I could someday give my child. I wanted to show our child how much we loved and wanted him or her, even before he or she was conceived. In the long run, the journal kept me sane and protected John from hearing every complaint as we walked from frustration and fear to contented faith.

I used a blank journal I picked up at a book store. The purple gerbera daisies on the front always made me smile when I wrote. Others who journal prefer using a password-protected file on their computer. Several software companies have program downloads available for journaling.

Another method to vent frustrations is an audio or video diary. Handheld digital recorders fit in a pocket or purse so you can record thoughts wherever you are. Most digital cameras come with a video feature, so there is no need to invest in an actual video camera for your diary. Just set the camera up on a table or tripod and hit "record."

The point is to relieve your stress a bit and collect your thoughts in a manner that won't cause additional pain to your spouse, family, or friends. Once you have ranted in writing or downloaded your discontent, you will be able to approach tender subjects more rationally. Some things you post to your journal will never go farther than its pages.

According to Pam Clary, licensed clinical social worker and social work field educator coordinator at Missouri Western State University, journaling is an excellent way to help a person process thoughts and feelings. "For someone to whom writing does not come easily, the thought of sitting down and journaling may not be appealing," she said. "However, I often suggested and encouraged this technique to my clients."

She has even applied the discipline of journaling in her own life.

About two years ago, I found myself in a physical, emotional, and spiritual environment that was outside my comfort zone. I sat down at the computer one day and began writing whatever came to mind. I didn't worry about spelling or grammar. I just typed. Words came rushing out. It felt good, and I began looking forward to my journaling time. I never wrote for more than ten minutes. Then I finished each entry with a section on blessings I had received. This forced me to see the gems that God was giving me, even though I felt something different. I always found something to write in the blessings section.

I learned that my feelings were mine and that I didn't have to feel bad for having them. By writing about my feelings, I was able to get them out, and this released me from some unnecessary emotional baggage that surely would have spilled over into my work and home life.

I began journaling daily two years ago. Now I occasionally go back and read parts of previous entries. It is amazing to see how I have grown spiritually and emotionally in that time.

I am surprised how quickly I forget the blessings in my life. Rereading my journal helps me remember that during a very difficult time God carried me. It's like the "Footprints" poem in my own life.

Clary points out that the feelings expressed in journaling are not necessarily the feelings that should be used in decision-making.

Figuring Finances

Most infertile couples feel there is no price tag too high when it comes to having children. Unfortunately, our emotions and our bank accounts are not always equally fortified. When the quest to have a child ends, even after reaching the point of contentment as a childless couple, there may be a tremendous amount of debt to deal with.

Debt is one of the leading causes of trouble in marriages. This is especially true if one spouse wanted to pursue treatment more than the other. When treatments result in nothing but unmanageable co-pays and collection notices, the pinch can traumatize more than your pocket book.

To avoid a breakdown over money, talk about the debt incurred during infertility. Decide together the best way to handle creditors and payments. The good side of medical debt, in most cases, is that as long as you are making reasonable payments on a monthly basis, most providers will be patient with you.

Keeping your marriage intact requires a foundation on the Lord. Successful couples seek God in everything they do. It doesn't take long for a relationship to disintegrate when we take God out of the equation. When John and I were both retreating from communication with each other, we also stopped praying and reading God's Word together. Taking our relationship out of fellowship with the Lord left us both vulnerable to attacks on our marriage. We were still attending church and praying individually, but even our individual study of the Bible waned when we weren't doing it together.

In the heat of battle it's difficult to stop and pray or stop and read the Bible, but those are the most powerful tools Christians have. When we make our marriage vows, we are not only pledging before one another "to have and to hold, for better or worse, in sickness and in health." We are also pledging that vow to God. Doesn't it then make sense that we include Him past our vows? A cord made from two strands breaks much more easily than a threefold cord. We have to remember the first and most important individual in our marriage relationship is Jesus Christ.

Return to Romance

It was one thing to accept our lives without children, but bringing intimacy and love back into our home was more difficult. For years we equated our desire for one another with our desire for children. The thought that my body was rendered useless by disease made it difficult for me to be close to John. I pulled away from his attempts to be physically intimate. Eventually he just quit trying, and our relationship became even more distant.

Renewing the romance in our relationship was awkward at first. Reproductive illness, hormonal changes, and stress cause physical changes that impact our desire to be intimate. After rejecting one another during the darkest days of our marriage, it was difficult to find the way around the automatic emotional roadblocks.

The light bulb moment happened when we were moving from the home we had shared for nine years to the house John's parents built in 1948. I was going through photographs and ran across an envelope of forgotten ones from early in our relationship. We looked so happy. Memories flooded back. I wanted to feel that kind of love again.

Thinking about the early years of our marriage made me smile. I made a list of things we did together that made us happy back then. It seemed so simple to be in love, just being together, laughing and enjoying our life together. I thought about how I treated John. When we were first married I waited for him to come home, makeup on, the house clean, dinner waiting. Had I done that in recent years? I had to admit that after hip surgeries, cancer, and life got in the way, I stopped doing many of the little things that told him I loved him. I became so focused on becoming a mother that I forgot to be the wife John needed. He lost sight of the woman he fell in love with and became burdened by a process that seemed to have no end.

That day, I decided that the move to his childhood home would be the turning point in our life together.

To bring halted romance back to life, think about the things you did before infertility took control of your marriage. Start to treat one another as you would if you just met. At first it can be difficult to put history aside, but when you greet him at the door dressed to impress just because you are happy to see him, he will feel important in your life again. Tell him that you love him the way you did when you were younger. You don't have to have fertility to enjoy romance.

When John saw how much I cared about him, it renewed his interest in spending time with me. We started having fun together. Summer days on the river, winter evenings watching an old movie, even working together on the farm in the spring and fall became flirtatious and exciting. The spark of romance brought us to the relationship we longed for. It wasn't forgotten after all.

My beloved responded and said to me, "Arise, my darling, my beautiful one, And come along. For behold, the winter is past, The rain is over and gone. The flowers have already appeared in the land; The time has arrived for pruning the vines, And the voice of the turtledove has been heard in our land. The fig tree has ripened its figs, And the vines in blossom have given forth their fragrance. Arise, my darling, my beautiful one, And come along!" (*Song of Solomon 2:10-13*).

We will go through winters in life. When the storm has ended, it is time to rise—not only to be reunited in love with our spouse but also to renew our relationship with the Lord.

Everything comes in due season. When your marriage has come through the winter and you are following God's leading for your life together, you will see a time of new growth. The sweet aroma of the Holy Spirit in your home and a harvest of fruit you never expected are just ahead.

Arise, for God is faithful. His plan is about to unfold new blossoms in your life.

Dear Lord, thank you for the spouse you have given me. Thank you for the purpose for which you created this union. Show us your will and your way as we walk in your path for our life together. Lord, we ask for your compassion for one another. Give us the passion that you placed in our lives the day we committed to life with each other and you. Bless us with understanding and commitment. Let our marriage be glory to you in every way. In Jesus' name. Amen.

6 DEVELOPING HEALTHY RELATIONSHIPS WITH BORROWED CHILDREN

Train up a child in the way he should go, Even when he is old he will not depart from it.

—Proverbs 22:6

Healthy relationships with "borrowed" children can be one of the most rewarding parts of your life, even when you cannot have children of your own. Nieces, nephews, and your friends' children allow us to look at life with unjaded innocence. Everything is new and exciting through the eyes of a child.

Surrounding our lives with the unconditional love of children is not only therapeutic but also allows us to reinforce the love of Christ in the heart of a child.

Relationships with children are sometimes difficult for childless couples. The emotions that surface while spending time with children who are not your own are strong and often overwhelming. Allow yourself to accept your emotional response and grieve for your lost dreams. When you begin to heal from your loss, you will be able to establish a healthy response to children in your life.

Some of the traps that prevent healthy relationships with other people's children begin with judgment of the parents. Remember that everyone has a slightly different parenting style. Respect the rules and discipline policies of parents to provide support for family members and friends. Resist the temptation to give parenting advice unless they ask your opinion.

It is tempting to preface your ideas by acknowledging your lack of parenting experience. In most cases that is a defense mechanism to prevent the information from being tossed back into your face. You do not need to state the obvious. In doing so, you may invalidate the assistance needed by the parent. If the parent asks for your help, he or she truly wants your advice. He or she knows that you do not have children but trusts your godly wisdom—and knows your heart for his or her child.

When John's friend Jack was looking for a car for his teenaged daughter, he asked John what he thought of a little red sports car Jack was about to purchase. John didn't think it was wise to give a sixteen-year-old girl such a sophisticated vehicle. He shared his opinion, and Jack bought the car anyway.

To avoid hard feelings over your time with other people's children, follow a few basic guidelines.

- Ask parents for permission before taking their child to a movie, theme park, or event.
- Respect time boundaries, and return at the specified time.
- Speak positively about parents to their children.
- Avoid the urge to allow children to load up on junk food and sweets while they are in your care.
- Call parents immediately if their child becomes ill or has an injury requiring more than a Band-Aid.
- Inform parents about altercations with other children, minor falls or bumps, and behavior that took more than one request to correct. These issues could be important at home later.
- If a child confides in you about trouble at home, do not belittle or bad-mouth their parents. Instead, speak to the parents and see if there is some way to help.
- If a child confides abuse in their home, you can report it to authorities anonymously through your local abuse prevention hotline.

John resisted the urge to say, "I told you so," when Jack's daughter sideswiped a guardrail trying to see how fast she could drive on the highway. Thankfully, she was okay, but the repaired sports car went toward the down payment on a sedan.

Generally, relationships with children of any age should not be separate from your relationship with their parents. In the case of teachers or organizations such as Big Brothers and Big Sisters, there will be boundaries placed by the administration. By respecting those boundaries, relationships are likely to remain intact. You cannot make a "borrowed" child your own. Parents who see healthy relationships between their children and other adults appreciate the value for their children.

When children are well-cared-for and happy and parents are involved in their lives, it is easier to have a healthy relationship with appropriate boundaries. Relationships with children who have been abused or neglected are more difficult. These are the children who cause us to ask, *Why? Why would God give these beautiful children to people who neither want them nor care for their well-being?*

Unfortunately, there is no answer to that question this side of heaven. This is where faith comes in.

We know that God sees things in our lives differently than we do. He knows the future, and His understanding is perfect.

"My thoughts are nothing like your thoughts," says the Lord. "And my ways are far beyond anything you could imagine. For just as the heavens are higher than the earth, so my ways are higher than your ways and my thoughts higher than your thoughts" (*Isaiah 55:8-9, NLT*).

It is vital that we trust God in these situations. Even in our childless state, God has a bigger plan for our lives and for the children with whom we have influence. Often what we see as abusive parenting on the outside is a result of exhaustion or godlessness. If we look at our childlessness as an opportunity rather than a curse, it is possible to make a difference in the lives of children every day.

Rebecca is single, never been married, and never had children. She is in her early fifties. As Rebecca realized she would not marry, at least not in time to start a family, she wondered if she should have made different choices in her life. Along with the stigma sometimes associated with singleness past thirty, people question her about her lack of children.

"I really thought that was common sense," she laughs. "If I don't have a husband, there's no reason to think I would have children."

Putting the state of morality in today's world aside, Rebecca said she enjoys other people's children and her own nieces often.

Rebecca worked afternoons in the library system for an elementary school district. She spent every day with children and never tired of their joy. What she did tire of were the signs of neglect and abuse that she saw and had to report occasionally.

"I was really becoming bitter toward people who parented badly," she said. "But then I met Kacee, and I saw a different side of the coin."

Rebecca told this story about a little girl she would have taken from her mother's home, based on circumstantial evidence.

> Kacee was walking down the street dirty-faced, with a diaper that needed to be changed. She was not even three years old. I called the police. Officers took Kacee to a safe place until her mother could be located. On the surface, this case looked like neglect.
>
> It was about two hours before Laura, Kacee's mother, called the police. She was frantic. Her child was missing. Laura was married, her husband deployed to Iraq. She was working nights and sleeping during the day. Laura's sister watched her four children while Laura worked and slept. However, that day she could not be there. Laura put the kids down for a nap, and after they were asleep she lay down to get some rest as well.
>
> Kacee and her older sister weren't quite as asleep as Laura thought and decided to go outside and play. When her six-year-old sister remembered she would be in trouble for going out without permission, she tried to get Kacee to go back inside with her. Kacee refused. She was having too much fun playing in the sandbox in the yard. Her sister went back in, sneaked into her room, and quickly fell asleep.
>
> Kacee apparently played for a few more minutes and then went to look for her sister. She couldn't open the door, so she started walking down the street in their neighborhood.
>
> Laura was not a bad mother, but seeing Kacee alone and dirty made me think she was. My first thought was that I would never

let my toddler away from the house like that. I thought her mother must be a lazy, selfish woman who cared little about her precious child.

When I found out the actual story, I felt terrible. My jealousy and judgment toward a woman I did not even know scared me. But what could I do? I didn't know Laura, and I had judged her unfairly. I felt convicted and decided to visit Laura to ask her to forgive me.

As I approached her door, I had no idea what I was going to say. I didn't have a chance to knock; she opened the door, already knowing I was the one who had called the police for Kacee.

"Thank you so much," she said with tears in her eyes. "I don't know what I would have done if something had happened to her. I owe you so much. I am so glad another mom found my baby girl. I know you understand."

I was surprised at her reaction and felt endeared to her. I told her I was not a mother, confessed my snap judgment, and asked for her forgiveness. She said she thought the same things about herself. She was so thankful and surprised the authorities gave Kacee back to her without an investigation.

We spent a long time together that day. Kacee and her siblings ran in and out, playing within their mother's sight. Laura shared her story and her longing to make friends.

She hadn't lived in the area long, and the only person she had for support was her sister. But her sister was only there temporarily to help her with the children. She was in college and would have to leave in a couple of weeks.

Laura had never known the support of a church family, and with husband gone and her family hundreds of miles away, she felt very alone.

I invited her to church the following Sunday, and she accepted. I worked in the afternoons, so after Laura's sister went back to school, I watched Kacee in the mornings while the other children were in school. Laura was able to get some sleep, and Kacee was safe.

Laura's husband returned from Iraq, and they moved on to his next duty station. He retired from the Army a few years ago. As

Kacee approaches her thirteenth birthday, I am so thankful to be a part of her life.

It is important, when we do not have children, to reserve judgment and opinion. We cannot possibly know the inside story of every child throwing a tantrum in the grocery store or every parent screaming at a child in the park. We don't know what we would do in his or her shoes any more than he or she can know what it is like to want children so desperately and not be able to have them.

> It is imperative to report suspected abuse to authorities to protect children. Reporting does not equal judgment. The day Rebecca called the police for Kacee did not condemn Laura—it allowed God to work in all of their lives. If you suspect immediate danger to a child, call 911 without hesitation. If you are seeing a pattern of signals that makes you think there might be abuse, you can call anonymously to report your suspicion. A child's life is worth the risk that someone will be upset that you called.

In order to develop healthy relationships with borrowed children, we must be healthy in the way we look at our childlessness. Childless couples typically err on two fronts when it comes to other people's children. Either we reject them completely because it's too painful, or we try to replace the children we won't have with other people's offspring. Of these examples, neither is healthy for the childless couple or the children with whom they spend time.

Realizing that borrowed children must be returned to their parents in the same condition—or slightly improved—as they were when they stepped into our care is the key. Children who enjoy the blessing of many caring adults in their lives have a better chance of growing up emotionally and spiritually sound. Knowing that aunts, uncles, and friends of their parents have their best interests at heart and have a good relationship with one another provides stability. It gives children the sense of security they need as they grow up in a world filled with inconsistency and spiritual pitfalls.

John and I have enjoyed being an important part of my nephew's life. From the moment I found out that my brother was going to be a father, I fell in love with the child who would carry our family's lineage. It relieved me from the guilt I felt about not being able to produce a grandchild. No one pressured me to have children, but I felt badly that my mother was not a grandmother.

The first year he visited the farm, we knew there would always be a bond between us that was different from other kids in our lives. It's not that we love him more than our other nieces and nephews, but our relationship with him is special. Rowan looks like me; he acts the way I did as a child, and he loves our farm life. Rowan is God's gift to us. We won't have our own children, but we have a glimpse of what that would have looked like when Rowan is around.

My brother and sister-in-law were going through a tough time financially the first summer Rowan spent on the farm. With enormous child care fees, it was tough for both of them to work full time with a five-year-old. We offered to watch him for as long as they needed us that summer. They were thankful for the break, and we were thrilled to have him with us.

When Rowan stepped off the plane and into my arms, I knew we were in for a wonderful summer. He introduced me to the friends he met on the plane, and we headed for the luggage carousel. All the way home he told me about his plans for his vacation.

He filled his summer on the farm with chasing toads in mud puddles, running through fields with the farm dogs, feeding cattle, and discovering that it is best to stay away from a mama pig when she is in the mood to protect her brood of piglets.

We went to the YMCA for swimming lessons, enjoyed play dates with friends, and ate ice cream at our favorite sidewalk café. We had a great time getting to know one another.

John took Rowan fishing and taught him about combines and farm implements. Having him in our home brought out the best in us. It also made us think of what life would have been like with our own children. The question we buried long ago came creeping into our thoughts.

"Would we have been good parents?" I asked, knowing the answer I wanted to hear. John always told me I would have been a great mom, and I assured him he would have been a wonderful father. However, over the summer as I thought about that question, I realized that it didn't matter. The fact is that I am not a mother, and I will not be a mother. The question changed. It is important to be a good aunt, a good friend, a good mentor, and a good example to the children God places in my life.

Like most kids his age, Rowan is full of energy. He is an extremely bright little boy and can be a handful. Discipline at our house was something we had never had to think about. How would we discipline Rowan if he were our own child? Should that be different since he isn't ours?

I asked my brother what methods they found most effective with Rowan. He told me to use my judgment. "My son would not be in your home for two months if I doubted your ability to parent," he said.

It was the highest compliment he could give me. He trusted us to care for and nurture his only son. The responsibility to give Rowan the best aunt and uncle he could have was an amazing feeling. Part of that meant setting up house rules and giving Rowan boundaries in our home. Being the house of fun does not necessarily establish a healthy relationship with children.

Rowan pushed those boundaries. He wanted to see if he could change rules, skirt the edge of what was acceptable, and basically get away with a summer of free rein. He soon realized that the adults in his life are a team. If it is not acceptable at home or at Grandma's house, it's not acceptable at our house either. Working together, the adults in his life will help him grow up into a wonderful adult.

As we put Rowan onto his plane at the end of the summer, John and I finally had the answer to our big question. Yes, we would have been good parents. We could love a child twenty-four hours a day, seven days a week, even when the child was throwing a tantrum, not feeling well, or spilling his or her milk on the mail.

For the first time, we could see God's plan in action. There were opportunities for us to love borrowed children that would have been impossible if we had our own. God didn't decide we were not parenting material; He wasn't punishing us for personality flaws that might harm our children. He simply is working in our lives differently than He is working in the lives of other couples. In His omniscience, He ordained our childless marriage to be the summer haven for Rowan. He created us to be the teachers for Sean and the relief for people like Laura. We don't know how many other children God will place in our lives or what other doors of ministry He will open. We do know that His perfect plan doesn't leave us empty. It makes us available.

Debbie Buchanan spent her life loving children as an educator. Over the years, certain children have touched her heart deeply. Tyler was one of those children.

I hugged him for the last time, a long, tight hug. He had, in a way, been mine for the past nine months. He was entrusted to me to guide and teach so he could move on. Today he was leaving me behind.

My choice to be childless was a conscious one. My life was unstable and filled with depression during my childbearing years. I thought I would eventually get it together and there would be time for a family. By the time I was able to provide a healthy home for a child, too many years had passed. This left the place in my heart I had reserved for my children empty. The older I got, the bigger that empty place became.

As a teacher, each year I found a student or two who were intriguing to me. These kids did not have a good place to call home or were the kids who thought of school as nothing short of daily torture. While they were always special to me, I had managed to keep a safe distance between us. I needed to protect myself, because I knew they would move on. My heart had been broken too many times. Then Tyler came along.

Tyler was only eleven, but he had already been in the legal system. Trouble followed Tyler everywhere. School was a nightmare, a daily reminder of all the ways he didn't measure up. He cursed, spat, kicked, hit, and refused to work. He could barely read and write. He didn't know math, and he couldn't make friends. He was a little boy who desperately needed someone. I resolved to do all I could for him without letting him intrude into my life. After all, he would be with me for only nine months. I made sure I kept plenty of distance between us.

It was not easy to like Tyler in the beginning. He was disruptive to my teaching and the other students' learning. It seemed that no amount of reward or correction affected his behavior. In spite of my growing frustrations, something under that blonde hair and behind those blue eyes kept me awake. Night after night, I searched for the something about him that had me hooked. One night as I lay there with my emotions eating me alive, I realized that no one in Tyler's life ever cared enough about him to even give up on him. He was nonexistent in the world from which he came. Tyler was a child without a face.

I worked harder after that night to win Tyler's confidence. He needed someone to trust, but he had learned that trusting ended in being hurt. His answer was to keep people away, something I could certainly understand. I gave Tyler all the time I could give him without neglecting the other students. I had to show him there was someone in his life who would not hurt him.

Tyler and I made a behavior chart. I watched him carefully choose each crayon as he decorated the chart. He colored it quickly and recklessly, paying no attention to the paper's edge or the carefully placed lines. He covered the tabletop with crayon scribbles. I let Tyler color the chart, the table, and the soles of his shoes. I was not about to interfere. For the first time, I saw him focused and with a purpose.

Tyler put the adhesive stars on the chart. My plan was that he would start with all the squares filled. I wanted him to believe he already deserved the stars. As behaviors interfered with the classroom, he would remove a star. He needed to see the relationship between his behavior and the consequences he was receiving. The reward system I had tried certainly hadn't worked, so I was hopeful reversing the process would meet with success. The glue was barely dry on the last star, however, when Tyler saw one of the students looking at him and called her a name. The first star had to be removed.

I hadn't realized how difficult it would be to get Tyler to remove the stars. The name he had called the student was mild compared to the one he called me. I took him and the chart into the hallway. He screamed, swore, and threatened me, but we finally reached an agreement: if he would take off the star, I would give him a chance to earn it back. He thought that was fair. I wasn't sure, but it seemed worth a try.

Tyler earned that star back. In the days and weeks that followed, he lost many stars, but he worked hard to get them back. I watched him slowly change as he began to trust me. I began to trust him too. Stepping out into the hallway, leaving him without supervision, I watched him through the small window in the door, and I began to see him through new eyes.

Tyler's dramatic changes were affecting me. I looked forward to seeing him each day and marveled at his persistence in learning to read and write. I watched him develop friendships as he began to believe in himself. Even though I knew he was only on loan to me, I no longer kept my distance. Tyler was filling that empty place. He had grabbed my heart and was hanging on for all he was worth. For the first time in a long time, I was letting that happen.

The school year was ending too quickly. When it was over, Tyler's mother was taking him to another state, and I knew I would not see him again. Even as I grieved, I tried to make the most of the time we had left. I wanted Tyler to know how important he was to me. I took every opportunity to show him what a great kid he was.

When the school bell rang for the last time and Tyler was officially no longer my student, we spent that last afternoon eating pizza in the park. I told him that he had given me something I had wanted for a long, long time. I made sure he knew I would always remember him. He was twelve and embarrassed by my words, so he answered by asking how old I thought the tree across the road was. I could do nothing but smile and take a guess.

As we arrived at Tyler's house, I longed for nine more months. It was a selfish longing, for Tyler no longer needed me. He could read and write, he could do math, and he had friends. I had done my job, and he had done his. It was time for him to move on. I held him at arm's length and looked at him intently. Then I gave him the longest hug I had ever given anyone. However, as long as it was, it didn't feel long enough.

I worried about Tyler in the days that followed. I prayed that life would treat him well. He was still fragile and vulnerable. As the days passed, I began to accept that I had done all I could. He was out of my hands. Now it was up to him.

One day years later a letter with no return address arrived at school. I had seen the slanted, scrawled handwriting on the envelope somewhere before. As I took the card out, I saw the daisies on the front. Daisies were my favorite. My hands began to shake.

Dear Ms. Buchanan: I am twenty-one now, and I am fine. I just want you to know I am making my way in life because, when I needed it most, someone believed in me. That someone was you. I will always remember you and what you did for me. Thank you. Love, Tyler

As a tear crawled down my cheek, I felt so proud of him, so proud of us. We were making our way in life. We were moving on. *Tyler, my borrowed child,* I thought. *What more could I ask?*

Sometimes our borrowed children come when we are least expecting it. Our need to mother doesn't end at the time that our children would have been adults. Some of my most treasured borrowed children have been college students. Something about being childless makes us more trustworthy in the eyes of young adults. At an age when they are trying to gain independence from parental authority, they crave the advice and attention of people their parents' age.

My friend Jodi Thomas shared her experience with a son who was not her own. Jodi had been clinging to Psalm 50:15 from the *New Living Translation*: "Trust Me in your times of trouble, and I will rescue you, and you will give Me glory."

She just didn't know how the Lord was going to rescue her or where the glory would come from.

In the summer of 1995 I lost my fifth baby. I always hated to call my children pregnancies, because it somehow seemed to diminish the fact they were my children. While I was never able to carry a child past my first trimester, they were still my children. This time we knew it was the last attempt for my husband, Tom, and me to conceive. My last three pregnancies were ectopic. My doctor, with tears in his eyes, announced that he was not able to save any of my Fallopian tubes. Our only option would be in vitro fertilization. After much prayer, we both decided that was not a route we were willing to travel. Honestly, I didn't think I could bear another loss.

This grief seemed different. Probably because I had never really dealt with the pain from my previous losses; I was always able to try again. This time there was no "again." The pain was deep.

In this pain, I felt darkness between the Lord and me. I did all the right things. I attended church, tithed, asked the elders to anoint me with oil and pray for me. I asked—but I didn't receive. *Was it me? What happened?* Of course, I never let on with my church family. I always quoted the right verses to make people believe I was dealing with the grief in the proper Christian spirit. But I hurt.

My friend Jeannie told me about a ladies' luncheon called "Tea with Dee." Dee Brestin had spoken at her church. I was not able to attend, so she provided me with the recordings from the meeting. I listened to the entire service but still felt nothing but pain. Then something in my spirit changed. It was the closing prayer of the last tape. Dee prayed, *Lord, for those ladies who will be mothers, we pray your patience and guidance for their journey. For those ladies who will not be mothers, we pray you would change the desires of their hearts.*

What? Change the desires of my heart? That was my stumbling block. At that moment I got on my knees next to my bed and wept. *Lord, please change the desires of my heart. Help me to attend my friends' baby showers without leaving in tears. Lord, please help me to hold another woman's newborn without the deep ache. Help me, Lord, as only you can.*

Then Dee Brestin prayed the prayer that changed my life. *Lord, I will accept the fact that I will not be a biological mother. I will accept that I will not have an answer to why this side of heaven. But, Lord, when we meet, I want to know why you gave me the heart of a mother but not the body.*

Tom was a police officer when we married. As is common in law enforcement, it was a generational career. Tom's father was a police officer. Family stories report that the Thompson family roots in law enforcement date back to the days of outlaws like Jesse James. Rumor has it that Tom's great-great-grandfather was the sheriff who arrested the Ford brothers for the murder of Jesse James.

Tom had custody of his two young daughters. Jenny was seven, and Renee was thirteen. I immediately became a stepmom. The girls were not interested in law enforcement, and since I could not give Tom children, the family heritage in the field would end with Tom.

When Renee met Charlie, we never imagined how important he would become in our lives. He was a wild seven-year-old. We watched him grow into a good man, and when they married we didn't lose a daughter; true to the cliché, we gained a son. He and Tom worked out three days a week, every week. It did not matter what other plans we had—they always got in their workout first. I would knock on the weight room door and yell, "There is too much talking and not enough pumping, and we have places to go!" They responded, "No girls allowed!" It always made me smile.

When Charlie told Tom he was interested in law enforcement, Tom was elated. Charlie went on to the academy and became a sheriff's deputy. Charlie loved his job. Renee and Charlie blessed us with our first grandson, Trevor. Of course, the first gift to the new baby was a rattle that looked like a dumbbell and a police car.

On June 23, 2007, in the wee hours of the morning, we received the most dreaded call for a law enforcement family. I answered the phone to Renee's sobs. I could hear Trevor crying in the background. In slow motion I heard the words between her tears: "Charlie has been injured on duty. He has been taken by ambulance to the hospital." Another officer was with Renee to take her to the hospital. We met her there.

Tom went into what I call "cop mode." It was as if he were taking a report. "What happened? Where did it happen? Who was driving? How fast was he going?" On the way to the hospital, he took a different turn. I asked him where he was going, and he said he wanted to go by the crash site. The crash site—I couldn't believe my ears! I thought maybe he hadn't heard me, so I reminded him that the ambulance had already taken Charlie to the hospital. He said, "I understand that—I want to drive by the accident."

When we arrived, the road was still blocked off. He gently turned without a word, and we proceeded to the hospital. When we arrived, while still in the car Tom looked at me and said, "The boys are working the accident as though it's a fatality. I want you to know that before we go into the hospital."

Charlie had been involved in a high-speed pursuit. Another officer had requested assistance, and Charlie was the closest officer. He was in pursuit of a motorcycle when he topped a hill; there was a semi-truck turning in front of him. He swerved to miss the truck and hit a cement wall. His injuries were critical—his injuries had torn the aorta from his heart. Lifeflight took him to University of Kansas Medical Center in Kansas City, Kansas. After five long days, it became apparent his injuries would take his life.

I had just left Charlie's room. Renee wanted to be alone with her husband. Tom and I walked down the hallway, and moments later we heard the sobs. Charlie had crossed over into his ultimate healing with the Lord. I later explained the pain to a friend, saying it was as though the angel of death had sucked the life out of my body, but I didn't die.

Charlie's Aunt Julie was walking toward us. "It's over," she said quietly. "Jodi, you and Charlie were meant for each other. He needed a mother, and you needed a son."

At that moment, truly one of the darkest moments of my life, I heard the Lord's still, small voice. He answered my *Why?* from twelve years earlier. God spoke directly to my heart: *Now, Jodi, you know why I gave you the heart of a mother.*

It wasn't so much that God answered my question at that moment that blessed my heart so much. It was the fact that He wanted me to know that He never forgot my question. Personally, I believe it is more important to trust God than to love Him. Love is easy. Trust, on the other hand, has been very difficult for me. I have a learning disability. At fifty years old, I still cannot tell you what seven times eight is. I was never able to memorize the multiplication tables. While I have learned to work around the disability, I have always been saddened that I cannot memorize scripture. I prayed and asked the Lord to help me. I asked Him to heal that part of my brain. In His infinite wisdom, He instead allowed me to memorize *one* scripture. While I cannot give the reference without looking it up, my gift scripture is "I trust in you, O Lord; I say you are my God and my times are in your hands." I know why He gave me that scripture. For me, I cannot call Him "my Lord" if I don't trust Him first. I believe that nothing—nothing—comes to me that hasn't first passed the hand of God. I can say I trust the heart behind the hand. *Why* just doesn't seem as important.

Relationships with borrowed children may come into your life when you are thirty or when you are seventy. Either way, if you allow God to use you in the lives of others, you will be comforted in your own pain.

"Shout for joy, O barren one, you who have borne no child; Break forth into joyful shouting and cry aloud, you who have not travailed; For the sons of the desolate one will be more numerous Than the sons of the married woman," says the LORD.

"Enlarge the place of your tent; Stretch out the curtains of your dwellings, spare not; Lengthen your cords and strengthen your pegs.

"For you will spread abroad to the right and to the left And your descendants will possess nations And will resettle the desolate cities.

"Fear not, for you will not be put to shame; And do not feel humiliated, for you will not be disgraced; But you will forget the shame of your youth, And the reproach of your widowhood you will remember no more.

"For your husband is your Maker, Whose name is the LORD of hosts; And your Redeemer is the Holy One of Israel, Who is called the God of all the earth" (*Isaiah 54:1-5*).

Allowing the Lord to place divinely appointed children in our lives brings a different revelation for each couple. Letting go of the grief, guilt, and shame we once felt about not being parents has allowed John and me to enjoy Rowan and many other children in our lives.

Enjoy them and allow the Lord to minister to them through you. You may be the one they look to as an example of Christ's love.

Dear Lord, thank you for putting children in our lives. Help us to share your love with them. Lord, make us a support to their parents so that these children will grow up knowing how much a team of adults loves them. Give us wisdom to do your will in their lives. In Jesus' name. Amen

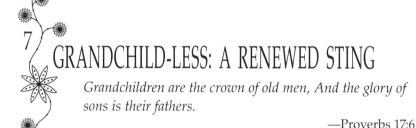

7 GRANDCHILD-LESS: A RENEWED STING

Grandchildren are the crown of old men, And the glory of sons is their fathers.

—Proverbs 17:6

By the time we are in our mid-forties and fifties, we know our chance of being parents has passed. The elusive concept of making peace with that reality has finally settled in, and we are ready to live our golden years without the debt of college educations and bailing out our adult children.

Relationships with friends that were once distant are often renewed as their children go off to college and leave them with an empty nest. They are finally free to have dinner and socialize with us after being shut out by play dates, school plays, and soccer practice.

My friend Renee always tried to make time to get together. It was a conscious effort that I appreciated. Her daughter, Lindsey, was very active in sports and academic events, but rather than beg off from doing things with me, she invited me to be a part of Lindsey's life.

When Lindsey left for college, Renee was beside herself. She didn't know what to do with her time or with the empty place in her heart that holiday homecomings couldn't fill. She had been such a good friend to me, and I was happy to be there for her. She needed a friend who knew what it was like to be alone.

Renee's husband did not handle the empty nest well. He retreated to the Internet, leaving her feeling emotionally abandoned and questioning their twenty-two years of playing happy family. Our situations were different, but I understood what was going on in her heart.

By the time Lindsey came home for the summer, Renee and her husband had adjusted to this new phase of life. Our friendship was stronger than it had ever been, and I was thankful that God made me available to her.

During Lindsey's tour through higher education, Renee and I met a couple of times every month to catch up. I enjoyed sharing the time with her and offering support as she watched her daughter change from a child to an amazing young woman. It was nice to have such a close friend, and I loved hearing Lindsey's collegiate adventures. I avoided thinking about the children I would not send off to college. It was another milestone journey that summoned the familiar, wistful feelings of what might have been.

When Lindsey graduated, I was facing forty head-on and preparing for an amazing decade. I was eager for what God was going to do in my life. My speaking ministry was in full swing, and I saw God changing lives before my eyes. I couldn't have asked for more.

After college, Lindsey married the man of her dreams. A few months after the wedding, Renee called and invited me to lunch. We hadn't seen each other since the nuptials, and I looked forward to catching up.

We met at our favorite café, hugging and giggling like much younger women. Over an appetizer of brie and fresh fruit, she shared the news that had her on cloud nine and put me on auto pilot: her daughter was having a baby. Renee was going to be a grandmother.

I wanted to be happy for her. I wanted to rejoice with her. I wanted to help her pick out shower invitations and offer to bake the cake. Lindsey was like a niece to me. I was her confidant when she couldn't talk to her mom. I helped her surprise her parents with a theatrical engagement announcement and went with them when they chose her wedding dress.

But momentarily I was frozen by a flood of emotion I could not express and a ton of expectation I couldn't handle.

I had never given much thought to grandchildren. I knew they wouldn't be a part of my life, but dealing with it seemed distant and unnecessary. If we had been able to have biological children, they would still be in elementary school, not giving me grandchildren. Yet here it was—the familiar sting of childlessness rearing its head again. Except this time we were grandchild-less. It was a slap in the face, reminding me that our family stopped with us.

I quickly regained my composure and hugged my friend. She was so happy, and I was not willing to take that away from her. There was no way she could know the effect her announcement was creating in my heart.

After lunch I went to the park and watched older adults with their grandchildren. They looked so happy. Three generations, or maybe four, gathered for a birthday party. I sat on a bench watching them, thinking, *What if?*

The finality of my childlessness hit me at that moment. Permanent infertility, the painful decision to accept John's refusal to adopt, and finally becoming content with the life God had given me should have prepared me for this part of the process. I didn't feel prepared.

Knowing our branch of the family tree ended with us, and understanding what that meant, hit me very differently. I hadn't given a lot of thought to grandchildren. Great-grandchildren never crossed my mind at all.

From the anonymity of the bench I watched a laughing, blue-haired lady in a lawn chair hugging and kissing the third generation that came from her body. The way they loved on her put a new perspective on the life I thought I loved.

Knowing that this scene would never repeat itself in my life made me jealous. Who would love me when I was eighty? Would I be invited to birthday parties for children who weren't obliged by blood to love me? Or would I be forgotten?

A hunched and silvered gentleman sat in the chair beside her. He took her frail hand in his, lifted it to his weathered face, and kissed it gently. The look of love and pride in his eyes as he surveyed the fruit of their many years together brought the acid of envy to my throat.

That evening I asked John if he gave any thought to the idea that we wouldn't have grandchildren. Two years younger than I, he said he didn't think he was old enough to worry about it. I told him about my lunch with Renee and my trip to the park.

He hugged me. "Everything God has for our lives up until now is in place," he encouraged. "We couldn't have expected grandchildren." He was right, but I still wondered if this new sting was going to keep threatening my heart as we got older.

John broke into my thoughts. "I know how hard it is to watch other people with their grandchildren." As we sat on the couch, he told me about his friend's grandson. "He calls me Mitter Johnny," he said. "I can see Rick in his features and his mannerisms. It's so funny to watch him watching his grandpa. He wants to be just like him."

We sat quietly for a while before John spoke again. "You know, nothing says we can't enjoy the time we get to spend with other people's grandchildren."

My pain subsided a bit, and I remembered how thankful I was for the husband God gave me to walk with through this journey.

There was so much we would miss in our golden years because we didn't have children. Until Lindsey's pregnancy, I hadn't thought much about it. The day Renee told me about the baby, my reaction took me by surprise. I was constantly seeking God's guidance in my life. He had changed the sorrow of not having our own children to joy for the blessings in our life. Yet in that moment I wanted nothing more than to grow old knowing that someone would remember me and love me. I wanted to matter fifty or even one hundred years after I was gone from the earth. My longing to be remembered reminded me of a neighbor we knew when we were young.

When John and I had been married just a few years, we moved from southern California to his hometown in northwest Missouri. We rented a house in a quiet neighborhood. The day we moved in, our elderly neighbor, Miss Ella, greeted us with a shoofly pie.

Miss Ella was ninety-six years old. She had lost her husband when she was seventy-two. For more than two decades she had lived alone. Her brother, Theodore, visited her as often as he could. Theodore was John's uncle, so we tried to keep an eye on Ella for him

Ella sat in her living room, gazing out at the children playing in the park across the street. At ninety-six years old, there was not much else to do with her day. I wondered if she regretted not being a mother.

My knock on her screen door startled her a bit. As she made her way to the door, I thought of how much she looked like the perfect grandmother. Curly white hair framed her face. Her wire-rimmed glasses were perched neatly at the end of her nose so she could see past the lenses to look into the distance. Her green polyester house-dress fit a little baggier than it had when it was new, probably thirty years earlier.

I returned to the kitchen the cake plate I had borrowed. After two years as a neighbor, Miss Ella was like a grandmother to me. We enjoyed afternoons of tea, and I loved listening to her stories from the twenties and thirties, when she was my age.

I made tea and settled in for a visit, but that afternoon something was bothering her.

"My husband wanted a son, you know." She said it quietly. I nodded, and she continued. "I tried everything to give him a baby, but there was just something wrong with me."

Miss Ella shared her story of infertility and regrets every couple of months. This time she took a different turn. "I'm glad he never figured this part out." She turned to the window, facing the children who were still playing across the street. "Not having children was hard," she said. "Not having grandchildren and great-grandchildren is worse."

Tears threatened the corners of sad eyes. "I'm older than all my friends, and I have lost them anyway," she said. "My only family is Theodore, and I guess also you and John since he married John's aunt, but besides the three of you, no one is going to remember me. No one will visit my grave, and no one will care about my house or my stuff when I'm gone."

I tried to tell her that many people cared about her, but she wouldn't hear it. We visited a little longer before she said she wanted to take a nap. I didn't know what to say or how to make her feel better.

I hugged my sweet friend and left. Instead of going home, I walked across the street to watch the games of tag and catch that caused her heart to break. I wondered if Miss Ella would be our neighbor when our children came along. I hoped that she would know them. Little did I know how much my life would mirror Miss Ella's in a few years.

As John and I went through the battles that led to childlessness, I never thought about Miss Ella's life and the mirror that mine was becoming. However, when grand-childlessness set in, I thought of her often. I pictured myself as a nonagenarian, alone in my rocking chair, wishing for what would never be.

Miss Ella brought so much joy to us and to others in the small community where she spent her life. People revered her for her sage advice and loved her for the thoughtful things she did for them. When Miss Ella passed away, the church was full. Five generations of neighbors came to say goodbye to a woman who thought she didn't matter.

Although her lineage ended with her, the impact she had on her community lives on. Miss Ella knew the pain of grandchildlessness, and it broke her heart.

God knows every generation from the beginning of time, and we found comfort in that. However, the emotions that came flooding to the surface with the realization that we would not have grandchildren had to be given release. Allowing ourselves to feel sorrow and express grief does not discount our faith. Nor does it change the fact that God is in control.

Reaching middle-age, grandchild-less, may bring old feelings to the surface. Feelings of loss and grief can be stronger as we age than they were in earlier years. Facing mortality, believing no one will remember you when you are gone from this earth, is devastating for some people.

The fact is, most childless couples give little thought to grandchildren during their early years of infertility. It doesn't cross our minds until it stares us in the face, bringing sequestered pain back into our healing hearts.

When our life together unfolded into a family of two, the perfection of the plan didn't end with our fortieth birthdays or the first grandchild among our friends. God's perfect love remains perfect. Allowing the enemy to disable us because of our lack of grandchildren would show the world and the Lord that our faith in Him is conditional and dependent on our emotional state.

Feelings last only as long as we allow them safe harbor in our hearts. When we are overwhelmed by new emotions, such as jealously, it is important to deal with them right away so they cannot take root and cause bitterness in our lives. Taking emotional inventory can reveal feelings we have not resolved and prevent the crippling effects of emotions gone wild.

To maintain healthy relationships with your family members and friends who are enjoying the pleasures of second and third generations, envy and fear must be put under the authority of Christ. Neither of these emotional responses comes from the Holy Spirit. They are natural responses, but that does not mean that we have to give them residence in our lives.

As the pictures came to my row, I debated whether I should pass them along or take the time to flip through the stack of chubby baby cheeks and delivery room portraits. Grandmothering was becoming a trendy obsession in my Sunday School class of middle-aged women. Every week another of my friends brought new pictures of her latest mini-me.

The stories they shared were even more precious than years earlier. The grandmothers could enjoy this generation even more than they had their own children. The celebrations were a welcome praise report, and I was thrilled for their complete joy.

As a childless woman, I missed rejoicing with my friends over their pregnancies and children. As a woman who is content—even happy—with what God is doing in my life, walking in His will and stepping through His open doors, I am able to be truly happy about their grandchildren.

I ran my thumb along the stack of photos I held. Slipping the first photo to the back of the stack, I couldn't help but smile—my friend's lipstick was evident on the baby's forehead in the next picture. As I pored over the pictures, I knew that everything was right in my world. I didn't have to become a grandmother to enjoy the grandchildren all around me.

Proverbs 14:30 says, "A sound heart is life to the body, But envy is rottenness to the bones" (NKJV).

When our contentment comes from the Lord and our joy comes from Him, our emotions do not rule our lives. Envy and fear cannot exist where faith resides.

God knows we are going to experience these emotions. He would not give us instructions about what to do with them if there were no validity to their existence. Just because emotions are real does not make them a safe place to dwell.

There is not a pain we can feel or a situation we can experience that He has not seen first. God knows sorrow, and He knows pain. He knows how loss feels, and He knows what anger is. It is not sinful to feel. It is, however, spiritually dangerous to give way to sin by allowing our emotions to rule our lives.

Isaiah 41:13 says, "I am the Lord your God, who upholds your right hand, Who says to you, Do not fear, I will help you."

No matter how alone we feel, the Lord is there, and He will help us through the times when we don't think we can keep going. Much of the help He offers in dealing with being without grandchildren is in the lessons learned years earlier. Remembering the peace that came when I let go of my desires and gave my heart's dreams to Him allowed me to enter this new phase with grace. I was already aware of the feelings passing through my mind, and I knew they were temporary.

Self-deprecating thoughts could not create the same apathy and depression they did before, because they were not welcome in my mind.

- Be aware of what you're allowing in your mind.
- Be alert for times when you find yourself dwelling on loss.
- Remember that thoughts come and go; don't place too much importance on a fleeting moment.
- Focus on Christ and your relationship with Him.
- Read the Bible, and offer praises to the Lord daily.
- Remember that you are a child of the King.

"The steadfast of mind you will keep in perfect peace, Because he trusts in You. Trust in the Lord forever, For in God the Lord, we have an everlasting Rock" (Isaiah 26:3-4).

No matter what you are going through in this season of your life, God will keep you strong. Our emotions come and go; our situations and circumstances flow in and out of our lives like the tide. Still, God remains faithful. He is the Rock upon which we can build our house. No matter what storms a life of childlessness brings, you are not alone.

Take comfort in the strength His Word brings. Remember: God does not have grandchildren either.

Dear Lord, we come before you filled with praise for the healing you have done in our hearts. We ask for discernment when floodgates of emotion sweep over us. Help us rejoice again with those who are rejoicing. Let us see the beauty in our lives without grandchildren. We love you and we trust your plan for our lives. In Jesus' name we pray. Amen.

8 LEAVING A LIVING LEGACY

Continue in the things you have learned and become convinced of, knowing from whom you have learned them, and that from childhood you have known the sacred writings which are able to give you the wisdom that leads to salvation through faith which is in Christ Jesus.

—2 Timothy 3:14-15

Have you ever thought about the legacy you leave as a childless couple? Some may think that seems absurd. *How can a family who ends with this generation leave a legacy?* The truth is—*everyone* leaves a legacy. No one who is born leaves this world without touching at least one other person. The footprint we leave on the world is our legacy.

You may not feel as though you are making a difference, but Scripture tells us that people notice what we do. In the Sermon on the Mount Jesus said, "Let your light shine before men in such a way that they may see your good works, and glorify your Father who is in heaven" (Matthew 5:16).

People are not listening to your words as much as they are watching your life. The way you handle life and the struggles you face marks the world's view of Christianity and can draw people to the Lord as you lift Him up in your life, or drive them away if you put yourself in the way of His glory.

As children grow up, they will choose people in their lives to emulate. The more positive examples they have, the more likely they are to behave positively. The impression of your legacy footprint creates a map that can lead to life in Christ or away from the shelter of His love. Where are you leading others through your reactions to your life?

Would you say that the apostle Paul left a legacy for the world? He did not have children. In fact, as far as we know, he remained single, dedicating his life to the Lord without a wife. Yet he mentored great men and women of God, wrote most of the New Testament, and is credited with being the first missionary known to Christianity.

If Paul had told the Lord he could not leave a legacy because he didn't have children, our world would be much different. But how did Paul come to ministry?

We read the story of God meeting Saul on the road to Damascus when he was still in the business of persecuting Gentiles who believed in Christ. Did he suddenly begin preaching Jesus to the multitudes? No. Another childless man, led by the Holy Spirit, went to find him.

> The news about them [men preaching the Gospel in Antioch] reached the ears of the church at Jerusalem, and they sent Barnabas off to Antioch. Then when he arrived and witnessed the grace of God, he rejoiced and began to encourage them all with resolute heart to remain true to the Lord; for he was a good man, and full of the Holy Spirit and of faith. And considerable numbers were brought to the Lord. And he left for Tarsus to look for Saul; and when he had found him, he brought him to Antioch. And for an entire year they met with the church and taught considerable numbers; and the disciples were first called Christians in Antioch (*Acts 11:22-26*).

Barnabas followed the leading of the Lord in mentoring Paul. Then Paul, once he had matured in the ministry, mentored Timothy.

Timothy already knew the Lord. Paul was not the one who taught him about Christ. Timothy benefited from the legacy of his mother and grandmother, who began a foundation of faith for their family. Like many of the children and young people in our lives, Timothy did not need parenting; he needed someone to show him the way to fulfill the calling God had on his life.

The legacy these men left to the world has survived for almost two thousand years. In the case of Barnabas, Paul, and Timothy, ministries sprung out of their deep faith and love for the Lord. They did not seek fame or self-promotion. They simply walked out their faith for the world to see. They followed God's plan and served Him with the gifts He provided.

When we follow God's leading in our lives, we will make an impact for the kingdom of Heaven on this earth. There are young people and children watching us every day. What message are you imprinting on their hearts?

Serve in the Church

"God has many ways to bless us with children to love and influence," biblical counselor Vikki Croutch explained. "Volunteer in your church nursery, Vacation Bible School, Sunday School, or evening programs."

During our time in children's ministry John and I saw many children come and go. Part of the ministry included a bus route through city neighborhoods to pick up children whose parents sent them but did not attend themselves. The opportunity to share God's love with children who might never hear the name of Jesus, except in anger, was an honor and a blessing in our life.

One evening we had dropped off all the children except Isabella. She enjoyed staying on the bus through the route and begged us to take her home last. Izzy, as she preferred, was thirteen. She was slightly older than the cutoff for elementary ministry, but because her family moved a lot, she was still in sixth grade. We loved her spunky spirit and enjoyed the questions she asked about God's love for her.

That particular evening she asked questions that were more specific. "How do I know if I'm supposed to be a missionary or somethin'?"

"Do you think you are?" I asked her. I wasn't sure how to answer her question. When I was thirteen I wanted to be a missionary every time we had a guest speaker at church. Since we had just studied about a missionary family a few weeks earlier, I thought her questions came from those stories.

"I think I'm supposed to tell people about God," she said. "Not like at school, but like all over the world. But I don't know how."

Over the next year, Izzy and I studied God's Word together on the van for the forty-five minutes it took John to deliver the other children to their homes.

Izzy was almost fifteen when she and her mom moved to Colorado. Her mom received Christ as her Savior just before they left, and Izzy stood by her side as she waited in line for baptism. If Izzy didn't know the joy of leading someone to the Lord before that day, she had a full dose as her mother followed her footsteps and changed the legacy of their lives.

I haven't seen Izzy since 2003, but I received a letter from her last summer. She is in her final year of Bible college, majoring in missions. Next fall she will leave for her first assignment with an international ministry. Izzy is taking the gospel all over the world.

In doing what you have been called to do, the Lord builds your legacy. Serving in the church gives you an opportunity to minister not only to children but also to their parents. I don't know how many times I have become aware of a young mother who stopped attending church because there was no one working in the nursery. Keeping children in the sanctuary works as long as they don't cry, squirm, or giggle.

Susan has four children under the age of five. She doesn't mind working in the nursery on a rotating basis, but she doesn't like being called in at the last minute on the weeks she isn't scheduled. She resents being blamed for the nursery being short-staffed. "I might as well stay home with my kids and avoid the hassle of getting them ready for church if I'm just going to sit in the nursery with them," she said.

Sometimes we childless couples think nursery duty is not our responsibility. That may be true, but the impact we can make on young parents of preschoolers could lay the foundation for families to stay in church as the kids get older.

There are many parachurch organizations that welcome believers to mentor teens and preteens in their programs. Volunteering as a camp counselor, working at the altar for youth rallies and programs, or serving behind the scenes helping with administrative tasks gives you the chance to be part of something larger than yourself.

If you feel led to work with such an organization, pray for direction from the Lord as you seek one that would be a good fit for you. If you are interested in a particular organization, ask for a statement of faith, and be ready to provide yours. It is important that the doctrine of the organization and your doctrine are a close match to avoid confusion for the children being served by the ministry.

Serve in Your Community

Organizations that are not necessarily religious in nature are a great way to be a positive influence on young people and your community. Big Brothers and Big Sisters, YMCA programs, the Boys and Girls Clubs, and the United Way all use volunteers in many of their programs for kids.

These organizations need both men and women as volunteers. Often the need for men is greater because of the demand for male mentors and the ratio of children to adults. If you are interested in any of these organizations, information is available online or by visiting your local branch.

Leaving a legacy in your church or community does not prevent you from creating a legacy in your own family. Staying in contact with younger members of your family gives you opportunities to influence their lives. As kids transition to teens to adults, having an aunt or uncle without children of their own can be a valuable asset to them.

"I love hanging out with my Uncle Rob," Jonathan told me. "He's my dad's big brother, but he's cool. He doesn't have any kids or anything, so he never had to get old."

Jonathan's perspective doesn't take into account that Rob spent thirty years working in the construction industry before he retired, allowing him to have a lot of time for Jonathan. Rob's wife couldn't have children, and when she passed away at the age of forty-three, he never remarried. His full life includes hunting, fishing, classic cars, and the Lord. He is a gift in Jonathan's life and in the life of his brother, Jonathan's dad.

Become the Family Expert

As the childless branch of the family tree, you may find it easy to feel as if everyone is growing past you. When our nieces and nephews were little, we loved visiting with them. They were happy to play games or just sit on our laps and be the center of attention at family gatherings. As they got older, we kept in touch, but their lives got busier, and we focused our attention on the younger sets of cousins who seemed more impressed and enamored with our photos of the farm and with our silly notes.

When my mother-in-law was sick, we lived on the farm with her. By not having children of our own to look after, I was able to stay home with her. I took care of her full-time for more than a year. When she passed away, I kept a treasure so special that I cannot help but pass it on to the rest of the family—I have her stories.

The legends she shared about family history, the documents she passed along to John and me, as well as the memorabilia she had saved when others called it trash created a time capsule of the heritage in our home. She saved postcards sent from her mother and grandmother, keys to their first cars, and the glasses they wore in the fifties and sixties. While there were many items her daughters and I cleaned out of the house, the treasure we sifted from her collections is a roadmap to their legacy.

After she passed away, family members came to visit just to see our collection of heirlooms and documents. The older folks added to the precious stories Virginia shared with me. The younger ones listened, eager to hear every story again and again. We scanned photographs and documents so they could have a record to show their children and grandchildren as their familial branches spread.

Our branch would never grow as long or as beautifully shaped as theirs. Instead, we would nourish them with the rich heritage that could have been lost. Being the family experts has given us something to offer. Our nieces and nephews, cousins and grand-cousins do not visit out of obligation or guilt; they actually enjoy their time on the farm. After operating for more than one hundred years, the family farm run by John and his bachelor brother is the only one in the family. Family reunions happen here, and generations of children run through acres of grass and open fields because we hold the beautiful stories of love and family that makes them who they are.

Some of the people who have been most loved by other people's children have themselves been childless. Theodor Geisel dedicated his life to writing stories for children, although he never had any of his own. When asked about his lack of heirs he said, "You have 'em—I'll entertain 'em."

Geisel wrote more than forty published books for children. His death in 1991 did not end the legacy. "Doctor Seuss," as Geisel is more commonly known, will remain on children's bookshelves for as long as the Lord tarries.

Hans Christian Andersen did not have children either. His effect on children spans more than one hundred years with stories like "The Steadfast Tin Soldier," "The Snow Queen," "The Little Mermaid," "Thumbelina," "The Little Match Girl," and "The Ugly Duckling."

Parents, teachers, and purveyors of classic literature worldwide celebrate Andersen's legacy of stories, bringing lessons of kindness and acceptance in the face of differences.

Another way to leave your mark on society is through scholarships, arts endowments, living trusts, and charitable donations. Choose your cause according to your passion. Your imagination is the only limit to the possibilities. Can you envision a student of the Bible going into the twenty-second century, receiving the scholarship you started before they were born?

Legacy is limitless. What is yours?

"Older women likewise are to be reverent in their behavior, not malicious gossips nor enslaved to much wine, teaching what is good, so that they may encourage the young women to love their husbands, to love their children" (Titus 2:3-4).

As we grow in maturity in the Lord, mentoring younger Christians is a great way to leave Christ's footprint on the world. When younger couples in the church watch you live for the Lord, it influences their families. Every marriage will face trials of varying kinds. Put yours at the foot of the Cross. When you turn to leave it there, you will see a line of people following your example.

In light of eternity, what matters most is whether others saw Christ in you and whether you pointed the way to Jesus and the eternal life He offers. Burnt offerings of shattered dreams become pure gold in the hands of the Father.

Dear Lord, thank you for loving me. Forgive me for calling myself useless and denying the perfection you created. Lord, let my light shine for you so that the thing most remembered about me is Jesus in my life. Show me ways that you would have me use the talents and treasures you have given me to bring glory to your name and impact the world for your kingdom. Father, make me a living legacy of your love. In Jesus' name I pray. Amen.

9 WHAT CAN YOU DO WITH AN EMPTY QUIVER?

Behold, children are a gift of the Lᴏʀᴅ, The fruit of the womb is a reward. Like arrows in the hand of a warrior, so are the children of one's youth. How blessed is the man whose quiver is full of them; They will not be ashamed When they speak with their enemies in the gate.

—Psalm 127:3-5

Growing up as the daughter of an evangelist, I believed that every scripture was written for me. I never considered picking the scriptures that I liked for my life and discarding those that didn't apply.

My favorite song as a child reinforced the truth of Scripture for me:

> *Every Promise in the Book is mine.*
> *Every chapter, every verse, every line.*
> *All the blessings of His love divine.*
> *Every promise in the Book is mine.*

Words and music by Thurlow Spurr, *Festival of Praise, Part II,* Copyright © 1978, Lexicon Music, Inc. Used by permission.

The words penned by Thurlow Spurr in that children's hymn were real in my life. I trusted that there was nothing in God's Word that wasn't mine.

As I studied the Bible during the surrender to our childless life, I began to see it differently. Certainly scriptures about children being like arrows couldn't apply to John and me. Would God not allow us to be well regarded in society if our quiver was empty? It seemed like a cruel joke that taunted me as I tried to find an application in our barren life.

I wished my dad was still a phone call away so I could seek his wisdom. I knew in my heart that my fears could not be truth. Yet there it was in black and white. The Word of God is truth—it does not lie. *If having a lot of children makes a man blessed in the gates,* I thought out loud, *then not having children must negate that blessing.*

I sat with that thought for a few moments, wishing I knew what my daddy would have said.

"You can't take one scripture and try to make it fit your life," I remembered his voice from years earlier. "You have to read God's Word as the whole, intact. Satan knows the Word, and he will twist the Scripture to defeat you if you let him."

I heard that more than once from the front row of many churches. It was part of the reason that I believed the entire Word was for me. We must not allow our walk with Christ to be hindered by a separated word.

I went back to the context of that scripture. Reading Psalm 127 in its entirety, without looking at the numerical divisions of each verse, I saw the context clearly.

> Unless the LORD builds the house, They labor in vain who build it; Unless the LORD guards the city, The watchman keeps awake in vain. It is vain for you to rise up early, To retire late, To eat the bread of painful labors; For He gives to His beloved even in his sleep. Behold, children are a gift of the LORD, The fruit of the womb is a reward. Like arrows in the hand of a warrior, So are the children of one's youth. How blessed is the man whose quiver is full of them; They will not be ashamed When they speak with their enemies in the gate (*Psalm 127:1-5*).

Scholars refer to this passage as A Song of Assents, of Solomon. We read in 1 Kings 3 that Solomon prayed and asked God to give him an understanding heart for the purpose of judgment. He was asking for wisdom—not for weapons, not for wealth, not for a long life—just wisdom. God blessed him with the wisdom he requested and much more.

"All the earth was seeking the presence of Solomon, to hear his wisdom which God had put in his heart" (1 Kings 10:24).

It was in that wisdom that Solomon wrote the passage we find in Psalm 127. It is not a passage that applies to one's children as much as it applies to our dependence on the Lord.

When I realized how complementary the message of these verses is to Jeremiah 29:11 and Psalm 37:4, I was thrilled. I began to look at other passages from a broader perspective as well. God's Word will convict our spirits of sin, but it will never harm us. We must not allow the enemy, Satan, to steal our joy by twisting scripture.

With that clarified, I thought about the "quiver of arrows" reference. John is an avid hunter. One year for Christmas I had a compound bow made for him. During the process the bowyer asked if I needed to speak with the fletcher. I didn't know there was such a craftsman to make the arrows in a particular fashion to fit their purpose.

He explained that *fletching* is the aerodynamic stabilization of arrows with feathers or plastic fins. The fletching is used to stabilize the arrow through air resistance in flight. Some fletches create spin when the arrow is launched. All fletches create drag on the tail of the arrow so that it reaches its mark without dropping to the ground.

As he spoke I envisioned the training of young people, parents teaching their children about the Lord so that they will one day fly with stability, hitting the mark wherever God sends them. It was a bittersweet moment as I wondered how we could send out fletched arrows when our quiver was empty.

A short time later I was introduced to Julie Ferwerda. We were both new faculty members with CLASSeminars (Christian Leaders, Authors, and Speakers Seminars) and attending our first training weekend. Julie and I were assigned to the same small group. As we shared our hearts for ministry in a roundtable discussion, Julie's story captured me. Tears came to my eyes as she described the project she and her husband were called to. She was writing a book called *One Million Arrows*.

Julie is recognized in Christian circles for making the Bible exciting and relevant to everyday life through her writing and speaking. Her articles have been featured in many Christian magazines and web sites for both adults and teens. Her résumé and willingness to serve the Lord were a blessing, but her dedication to an international orphan ministry in India piqued my attention. Her book is about more than orphans. It is about a ministry that fletches these children to be used according to God's purpose for their lives, even when they have no parents.

Shaping Children Beyond
by Julie Ferwerda

How about expanding your family this year?

Imagine for a moment that you decide to take in an abandoned child who needs a second chance at a purposeful life in Christ. So you adopt a baby boy from Africa. Say your efforts successfully sharpen this uniquely gifted young man as a faithful and empowered servant of God who devotes himself wholeheartedly to living and sharing the gospel (the mission). As he grows up, he decides to return to his native country as a missionary, and he leads many to Christ, many of whom begin sharing Christ too. Pretty soon, whole families become believers as a result, and they begin spreading the Good News within their communities. After a lifetime, the web of lives you've impacted for the Kingdom by that decision to parent an abandoned child is more than you could possibly have imagined.

Guess what? You can do this. Starting right now, you can adopt an orphan quite literally, or you can also ripple this kind of effect throughout the world without even going to the effort of actually raising a child in your home if you don't want to. Should actual adoption not be a good fit for your life circumstances, the hard work of gathering and raising them is already being done for you. Thanks to the many orphan ministries already in operation worldwide, including the United States, you can easily invest in the physical and spiritual needs of a child, regardless of your current situation!

Shaping beyond means looking outside your own situation or family for ways to invest in the mission through the lives of young people who need assistance. After all, every person and every family has the responsibility of The Great Commission—to go and make disciples of all nations. No exceptions. So why not invest in tomorrow's generation—the kids who could change the course of a community or a country?

As Americans, you and I without a doubt have the financial resources, with a little priority rearranging, to "go to the nations" with at least our money by investing in young people being shaped by many different ministries. While adoption of these kids is a great option that should be considered and explored, I'm also excited about investing in kids who are currently being raised up in their own cultures to bring lasting change through the love of Christ to their local villages, cities, and countries.

There are many great life-shaping ministries for children, both nationally and internationally. For work in other countries, I recommend investing in organizations that are shaping children through the means of special orphanages or homes—24/7 environments—designed specifically to develop children for the mission and to nurture them in all areas of life. Let me call your attention to a couple of great international networking orphan ministries devoted to every aspect of orphan care worldwide, the Christian Alliance for Orphans and Viva Network.

Closer to home, there are also many opportunities to invest in American kids doing short-term missions to other countries. This worthy investment helps interested young people develop a heart for the mission and gives them a chance to learn about other cultures. Many kids come from families who can't afford to send their kids on mission trips, but they still have the desire to make a difference and to use their God-given talents on the mission field.

One youth ministry drawing teens from all over the country for various aspects of ministry, Teen Mania, has a heartbeat "to provoke a young generation to passionately pursue Jesus Christ and to take His life-giving message to the ends of the earth." As a nondenominational ministry, it provides evangelism and service opportunities for preteens, teens, and young adult leaders on six continents for short-term trips. To date, they have taken more than 50,000 teen missionaries to fifty countries around the globe.

Youth with a Mission (YWAM) also began as a nondenominational youth missionary ministry but now includes all ages. They have operations in 160 countries and have more than 16,000 full-time volunteer workers in 1,100 locations internationally. They train 25,000 short-term missionaries annually.

What a great investment, keeping our young people engaged in the mission by helping them reach out to the world!

A very cool spin on investing in children, whether within or outside your own country, is this: you don't have to biologically reproduce in order to become a spiritual parent. Spiritual parenting can be just as meaningful and impacting as traditional parenting in matters of eternity, and can take on many forms. You can invest time, talents, prayer, money, possessions, and skills into shaping kids locally, nationally, or even internationally.

Spiritually parenting children who have no spiritual guidance or heritage is one of the most worthy investments of our time on this earth. By investing in as many children as possible in whatever ways we can, our spiritual offspring could potentially be limitless.

Kids on a Mission

In my work with orphaned and abandoned children in other countries, I've met children who are being shaped into disciples of Jesus by loving and devoted workers in loving, godly homes. These children have everything they need because of financial supporters, mainly in America, who are investing in them prayerfully and faithfully.

I believe these previously unwanted kids have been chosen by God to reap a great harvest of souls in their countries using their unique backgrounds, gifts, and passion for the gospel. Who's to say the child I invest in can't become a great spiritual leader in his or her country? Just think—you could invest in a young woman like Jennie.

Jennie

Jennie knows nothing about her South India parents except that when she was a newborn they threw her away and left her for dead in a city dumpster. Some college boys happened by and heard her crying, so they picked her up out of the garbage and took her to a nearby Christian orphanage, where she was raised into adulthood as a disciple of Christ.

Jennie was so bright that she graduated from Bible college at sixteen. Her instructors also noticed how mature and responsible she was at such a young age and how she had a heart for helping children, so they sent her to help out at an orphanage for younger children for one year of on-the-job training. When the main caregiver at that orphanage was called to another location during a time of need, Jennie took over. She was seventeen. For the past two years she's been taking care of an entire orphanage of eight younger children with the help of an assistant, Mary, who's now sixteen and also an orphan.

This position is a good fit for Jennie, who loves kids and feels privileged to serve them. "You don't have to give up everything you love to make a difference," she says. "It starts by thinking about others, then showing them the love that God has shown you. In this way He will use you to transform lives."

God is definitely using Jennie's love, experiences, and training to do just that for the little ones under her care. "When the children get sad and start crying for their parents, I can understand their pain and comfort them better than anyone else, because I've been in their shoes. I'm able to give the love and care they want and need, just like my caretakers showed me God's love when I was a child. I feel like a mother to them now."

Once an orphan now taking care of orphans, does Jennie have any regrets? "If I didn't know Jesus, I wouldn't be serving these children now. I'd be out living on the streets—if I was even alive." She believes that she will raise these kids to grow up and take care of others in the same way.

It's exciting to think how far-reaching your influence could be on a young life like Jennie's by spiritually parenting through financial support.

Lily

A thousand miles away in a remote tribal village of northeastern India, Lily is another young woman making a mark on the world. When she was thirteen, children in her village began showing up at her house during her visits home on school breaks, asking her to teach them. Boarding at an orphanage in a village some distance away from her home, just so she could attend school, Lily became the most educated person in her whole village, one of the few who could read. It was her dream to someday return to her village and open a school.

Now Lily is twenty-one, and her dream is becoming a reality. With high school and Bible college under her belt, she has moved back to her family's village, where fifty-seven kids come to her every day for schooling. The village families are so excited about this;

they have begun looking for some land where they can build a school for her to teach their children.

"The parents of the children believe in me and trust me to teach their children," says Lily. "They have been so encouraging." Sadly, this contrasts the opinions of her family and friends, who think Lily is too quiet and fragile to run a school by herself. "They don't know who I am on the inside," Lily confides. "I may seem unable, small, and weak on the outside, but I'm a very strong person on the inside."

Lily is most excited about how she will impact her village with the love of Christ. The first subject she teaches every day is biblical studies, and after school she offers a devotional time with singing and more Bible teaching. She says her students are enthusiastic in learning about God and the Bible. Eventually she hopes to start more schools in other nearby villages.

There are many like Lily who need faithful partners in order to bring Christ back to their own people. How amazing would it be for you to know you were helping teach fifty-seven kids in a remote village you'd never even seen?

Justin

Maybe you could also add a young man like Justin to your growing spiritual family.

After two years as a youth camp counselor, Justin decided to do something a little less dangerous—and more relaxing—than entertaining today's youth. He decided to become a Bible smuggler. At age twenty-one he went to work for Vision Beyond Borders, an organization that specializes in taking translated Bibles and evangelistic tools into the underground church in China and other parts of Asia, as well as Cuba, Turkey, Morocco, and Romania, with the purpose of equipping the local people for the mission. Currently this organization has hand-delivered more than 600,000 contraband Bibles worldwide.

Every three months or so, Justin tirelessly smuggles a backbreaking load of Bibles across borders on foot several times a day. He's had many opportunities to make a difference in the lives of believers who are hungry for the Word, as well as to see God miraculously open the way for him to get across borders under the noses of intimidating and suspicious border guards.

Without a doubt, Justin is making an impact. And while he has loving parents who are very supportive of his call to the mission, he's like the many other young people in our own country who could always benefit from having more adoptive spiritual parents who are willing to invest prayerfully and financially in his world-changing ministry. He has ongoing travel expenses, not to mention the ministry itself can always use more Bibles and teaching materials. In fact, when you invest in someone like Justin, you're taking the Word of God either into places it has never been or places it's not allowed, becoming a spiritual parent to many in the underground persecuted church.

Spiritual Parenting

Is the investment into these young lives worth it? Let the kids' lives speak for themselves. And it's never too late to get started making a huge difference. When you invest in a person like Jennie, you also invest in the eight kids she's raising to continue the process of hope. When you invest in someone like Lily, you also invest in the fifty-seven-plus kids who will carry the Good News back to their families and villages. When you invest in someone like Justin, you're taking the Word of God into places it's desperately needed, bringing light and hope to many in the underground, persecuted church.

Investing in mission-minded young people means becoming a spiritual parent, leaving a world-changing legacy for those you've never even met. You can personally play a role in impacting lives in villages, cities, and even countries, whether or not you ever set foot there. Now that is truly multiplication at its best.

To find out more about various orphan ministries—what they do, where they work, and how to get involved—go to <onemillion arrows.com>.[1]

Julie's ministry taught me firsthand that I can have a part in the fletching of arrows for the Kingdom, even when I don't have children of my own.

The words of a missionary I heard as a child still reverberate in my mind. "Not everyone is called to the mission field," he said. "Some are called to be the senders." The same admonishment applies to adoption. Some are called to be adoptive parents; others are called to give in other ways. If you are one of the couples called to adoption, you should absolutely be obedient to that calling. But if you are not called to adopt, it's okay to say no.

As a fletcher makes and sells his arrows, he knows he will never shoot the arrows that he so lovingly primes for usefulness. He doesn't see the prize, although he knows his skill and that his arrows are well prepared.

For the childless couple, this is great news. All of us, regardless of our family's size or economic level, can be a fletcher of arrows. If you can't afford to financially support an orphan ministry, you can become a mentor, a prayer warrior, or a teacher. Ask your church or local organizations how you can work with the children and youth in your community to make them strong and help them soar to the target for their lives.

Therefore I, the prisoner of the Lord, implore you to walk in a manner worthy of the calling with which you have been called, with all humility and gentleness, with patience, showing tolerance for one another in love, being diligent to preserve the unity of the Spirit in the bond of peace.

There is one body and one Spirit, just as also you were called in one hope of your calling; one Lord, one faith, one baptism, one God and Father of all who is over all and through all and in all.

But to each one of us grace was given according to the measure of Christ's gift.

Therefore it says, "WHEN HE ASCENDED ON HIGH, HE LED CAPTIVE A HOST OF CAPTIVES, AND HE GAVE GIFTS TO MEN."

(Now this expression, "He ascended," what does it mean except that He also had descended into the lower parts of the earth?

He who descended is Himself also He who ascended far above all the heavens, so that He might fill all things.)

And He gave some as apostles, and some as prophets, and some as evangelists, and some as pastors and teachers, for the equipping of the saints for the work of service, to the building up of the body of Christ *(Ephesians 4:1-12)*.

As Paul wrote to the church at Ephesus, they were dealing with discontented strife among the believers. Childlessness may not have been the issue, but nonetheless they had lost focus of their purpose. People wanted the same gifts that everyone else had and felt useless if they could not have them.

When we look at our empty quiver, it is easy to want the gift that the parenting world has. Staying true to the calling on our lives will reveal the ways in which we can be used to further the kingdom of God. In light of eternity, does it matter how many children we deliver from our womb or father from our DNA? To be useful in the Kingdom we do not need to produce offspring. But we *do* need to be obedient to the Lord.

Find your calling and your gift. Then use God's provision to fulfill His purpose for your life. He will give us a quiver so full of arrows that we won't be able to count the chances to make a difference for the kingdom of God.

Dear Lord Jesus, thank you for creating me for your purpose. Father, give me the opportunity to fill my quiver from the lives you put in my pathway. Help me to say and do the things that will keep your arrows aloft as they race toward the target. Lord, you are the fletcher, the maker and sender of arrows. I give myself to you. Use me, send me, and where I cannot go, help me to be a sender. In Jesus' name I pray. Amen.

10 PLANNING FOR THE FUTURE

The plans of the diligent lead surely to advantage, But everyone who is hasty comes surely to poverty.

—Proverbs 21:5

As an aging couple, we find that diligent stewardship of the blessings from God requires some planning for our future. Unlike most parenting couples, we must face the fact that we won't have the benefit of adult children to help us with daily care, special projects, and medical appointments as we age.

Even couples with children cannot always depend on those children for help. But we know now that we must be prepared for the future. Education about available services and programs will help childless couples avoid unpleasant surprises.

Daily Life

Most communities have senior citizen programs to assist with filling out confusing forms, finding reputable home repair companies, and providing low-cost or free rides to medical appointments and necessary shopping once we can no longer drive safely.

Everything you need to know about federal and state programs is at your fingertips. Visit the United States government web site at <http://www.usa.gov/topics/seniors.shtml>.

For services available through your state, do a search for senior services for the state in which you reside.

Resources in other countries are online. The European Senior Citizens Union can be accessed at <http://www.eu-seniorunion.info/en/organization/index.htm> and outlines services in more than twenty European countries. Many other countries have similar services. Doing your homework and staying current with available programs will make the transitions easier when you need to take advantage of assistance.

Meet Your Neighbors

In the busyness of everyday life, it is easy to ignore one of the best resources we have available. Our neighbors are the closest contact in case of an emergency, yet many of us don't even know their names.

One of the toughest realizations for me as I approached middle age without children was that no one would notice if I disappeared from the earth. While that may be a touch dramatic, the idea that no one would be calling me to see if I was okay when I reached my seventies and eighties caused me to feel extremely lonely.

I call my own mom every day. Before John's mother required full-time care, we checked on her on the way to work and again on the way home. When her health deteriorated and she could not take care of things on her own, we changed our living conditions to care for her at her home for her remaining years. Thinking of the times I took my precious mother-in-law to the emergency room because of a fall, or helped my mom deal with modern technology, made me think about who we would have to help us with the same things as we age.

All of the young people who have been a part of our lives will have their own parents to consider when that time comes. Will they have time to keep up with their old aunt and uncle too? They love us, and they are likely to check on us once in a while, but who will notice if we suddenly don't come out of our house for a week?

Building relationships with neighbors cannot wait until we are elderly. While we are young enough to contribute something to their lives, we should.

I have mentioned our beloved neighbor Miss Ella in an earlier chapter.

Ella was a wonderful neighbor. Although she was in her nineties when we moved next door to her, she made a point to meet us. She was kind to us and offered her wisdom and her smiles freely. As time went on, we expected to see Miss Ella puttering in her yard or rocking on her front porch. If a day went by that we didn't see her outdoors or have a call from her, we instinctively checked on her.

In the winter as John shoveled a path in our driveway, he often created a walkway for Miss Ella between her front porch and her mailbox. We didn't spend a lot of time with her, but we cared about her and we noticed her. For several weeks after she passed away, I still glanced to the south, expecting to see Miss Ella on the front porch.

Her kindness to us was not out of desperation to have someone care for her but rather a natural process of being a good neighbor.

What can you do to meet the people living in your neighborhood? Do you have a special skill or talent you can share with them? Have you ever thought of baking cookies to take to the families around you? Conversations are the first steps toward friendship.

Starting neighborly habits before you need those friends is a great way to be sure someone cares as you age.

Stay Involved

With the help of social networking sites like Facebook and Twitter, staying involved in family life is much easier today than it was even ten years ago. Keeping up with the nieces and nephews and their children gives them an opportunity to know you. When they see your excitement over special moments in their lives, it will be fun for them to include you.

The temptation for childless couples is to remove themselves from family events or to stay on the sidelines. Taking a backseat in the family serves only to separate you from loving relationships the Lord has put in your path. Being a family of two does not label you as a subfamily from whom others keep their distance unless you create an atmosphere that shuts them out.

It is easy to fall into the separation trap. When John and I were first married, we attended birthday parties for the children of friends and family members. The more we remove ourselves from people, the lonelier our childless state will be.

Keeping relationships open with family members, even when it's tough, ensures that we will not grow older alone. When we pour into the lives of others and love them with the love of the Lord, it will come back to us.

Research Contractors

Most of the time, younger family members don't mind helping with minor repairs and small errands for an aunt or uncle in need. Let them know how much you appreciate it. For larger jobs you will likely be more comfortable using a handyman or contractor.

Don't wait for your roof to leak before finding a roofer you like. It is easy to be taken in by scams when we seek help during a crisis. Make a list of services and contractors you know personally or by reputation. Meet with them briefly and ask for references. When you have a problem, it is nice to be able to call your trusted plumber instead of a shot in the dark from the phonebook.

Be sure to ask for a contract, even for small jobs. Anything your contractor says he or she will do for you should be in writing along with the agreed-upon fee.

Finances and Estates

Planning for the future, especially in areas of personal finance, makes many Christians uncomfortable. While it's true that we are not to worry about tomorrow, what we will eat or what we will wear, there is wisdom in reasonable planning for the years beyond our prime. There is a great difference between worry that causes fearful living and preparation for using God's resources and blessing in a responsible manner.

Our planning should follow the pattern and teaching in the Bible and put godly wisdom into practice. For example, there is no scripture that says specifically that you should create a will. But it's still a wise thing to do. Is there a specific Bible verse that tells us to update our résumés? No, but that doesn't change the validity of the advice. This concept is not exclusive to finances or future care. There is not one biblical reference that says to buckle our seatbelts, yet we know it is a smart thing to do. It does not mean that we trust the seatbelt more than God. But it is putting something provided for us by God to the best possible use.

There are many Scripture verses that show us how important it is to use wisdom and forethought in handling our affairs.

The naive believes everything, But the sensible man considers his steps (Proverbs 14:15).

There is precious treasure and oil in the dwelling of the wise, But a foolish man swallows it up (Proverbs 21:20).

The prudent sees the evil and hides himself, But the naive go on, and are punished for it (Proverbs 22:3).

Clearly, we are to use wisdom in planning our lives, even while we follow God's plan. Truly, planning does not equal worrying. In fact, not planning generally causes more worry and fear in our lives than an insurance policy or estate plan.

While most of our friends have been building college funds and saving for their children's first car or fairytale weddings, John and I were paying off medical bills, giving little thought to future expenses. There was a degree of freedom in thinking that we might buy a boat instead of the first semester at a private university. We didn't see an immediate need to worry about things that were a long way off, like nursing homes and our estate.

Retirement was a consideration. We had set up a few accounts to be sure we could afford to live without struggling as we reached our golden years. As a family of two, we didn't think it was important to consider what we wanted to happen to our stuff or any money that might be left.

John's brother, Otto, is a bachelor. He has never been married. Appropriately, he also has no children. After his and John's mother passed away, he decided he should think about his own estate and final arrangements. He is considerably older than John, but initially his planning made me uncomfortable.

"I don't have any children or anyone to take care of things—I need to do it now." He explained.

His planning caused John and me to start thinking about our own need to deal with our future as a childless couple. We hadn't given much thought to elder care, estate planning, or funeral arrangements. It was time to look ahead.

We visited our insurance agent, a financial planner, and the funeral home. The idea that was repeated by each of them was choice.

"You can wait until you're older or in poor health," insurance agent, Rae Laflin said. "But you will limit your choices and possibly allow the state to control what happens to you." Rae knew that our lives had been plagued by childlessness that we didn't choose, so he thought we should have choices about our twilight years.

Long-term Care Insurance

Rae explained to us that age shouldn't be a determining factor in needing long-term care. About sixty percent of individuals over age sixty-five will require at least some type of long-term care services during their lifetime. Purchasing long-term care insurance at a younger age is less expensive than waiting, and it puts the policy in place in case something happens. Once a change in your health occurs, long-term care insurance may not be available. Early onset (before age sixty-five) Alzheimer's and Parkinson's disease are rare in younger adults, but if either of these debilitating conditions is diagnosed, most insurance companies would deem you ineligible for new long-term-care policies. According to research by the United States Department of Health and Human Services (HHS), about forty percent of those receiving long-term care today are between eighteen and sixty-four years of age.

This type of insurance not only covers nursing home care but also provides benefits for home care in the event that a doctor determines it necessary. Each company has slightly different criteria to define medical necessity, but in general if someone cannot perform one or more of about six basic living tasks, he or she qualifies for some type of long-term or in-home care. The six most common criteria to receive policy benefits are bathing, continence, dressing, eating, toileting, and transferring. If you are unable to perform any of these tasks, or if you require substantial supervision to protect yourself from threats to your heath and safety due to severe cognitive impairment, your long-term care insurance will help you pay for the costs of care.

Without long-term care insurance, the cost of providing these services may quickly deplete your savings. Many senior citizens find themselves dependent on state assistance, leaving them with few choices for their care and possibly revoking the choices already made for their twilight years.

According to HHS, most health insurance plans provide for in-hospital care, doctor visits, and preventive healthcare needs. They are not likely to cover many other health-related needs of older adults such as the costs of long-term care, which is also not covered by Medicare.

Long-term care costs vary from state to state and are also affected by whether the area is urban or rural, but national averages reveal that the average monthly costs go up each year. To determine the best course of action in planning for your future long-term care, visit with your insurance agent or financial advisor. They are the experts in these issues and can guide you to the policies or methods that will best serve your needs.

HHS has developed a resourceful planning kit and a consumer web site to help you start looking toward your future healthcare needs. The kit is free, and you will not be asked to purchase anything, nor will anyone call to try to sell you anything. You can get this free kit and find resources to start the planning process on at <www.long termcare.gov>.

Life Insurance

No one likes to think about the end of his or her life. Even with the promise of salvation, death is a sad event to consider. Yes, we can know we are going to be in heaven with the Lord, and our loved ones can be assured that we are securely in the arms of Jesus. There is still sadness associated with the loss of a loved one.

As John and I planned our financial future, it seemed futile to worry much about life insurance since we don't have children to think about. Our financial planner suggested that we consider a minimal amount of life insurance to cover final expenses and help the surviving spouse through the first several months of bereavement.

When determining life insurance benefit amounts, experts advise thinking about what the money will be used for. Funeral and burial expenses, outstanding debt, income replacement, and legacy are possible considerations. In 2001 the average cost of a funeral in the United States was $6,130. Today the costs have increased by as much as fifty percent. The average cost of a basic funeral and burial in the United States is around $10,000.

During the grief process it is helpful for your surviving spouse to have a bit of a cushion to help with expenses. If you are the primary breadwinner, the amount of your life insurance should replace that salary for two years. If your household does not depend on your income, then a year's worth of wage replacement is appropriate.

Finally, consider any debt you have or payments you are making with your income. Debt will be inherited by your estate just as assets are. Having enough life insurance to pay your creditors will ensure a smoother road for your beneficiaries.

It may seem unnecessary to consider beneficiaries when you expect to be survived only by your spouse, but making plans for the worst-case scenario allows extended family members or friends to know your wishes before it's too late.

Life insurance can be designated to any person you choose. Your primary beneficiary will likely be your spouse, but a second designation is important in case your spouse does not survive you.

You can assign the benefits from a life insurance policy to your funeral home with instructions for them to give the remainder to your designated heirs. You may also have the insurance proceeds put into a scholarship account or trust for siblings, special causes, or nieces and nephews. Having a conversation with your insurance agent or financial planner will make your choices in life insurance easier.

Your Will

I remember the first time I was aware that my parents had a will. I was ten years old, and my mom thought it was important to tell me what to do in case something happened to her and my dad. I knew who to call if both of my parents were in an accident, and I knew where all the important papers were kept. It may seem like a lot of responsibility for a child, but I didn't really expect my parents to die—I just filed it in the back of my mind.

Having that information about my parent's final affairs led me to believe that people with children had to have a will. Since we didn't have children, a will didn't enter my mind for years. It seemed unnecessary and rather depressing.

In 2007 the will of a rich woman who left twelve million dollars in a trust for her dog made international headlines. We didn't have millions of dollars to leave to anyone, but we did have two dogs. We wondered if we should at least be sure there was someone who would take them in if we weren't able to care for them.

We decided to bequeath our critters to John's brother if he survives us. If not, they will go to my brother. It may seem silly to make those kinds of arrangements for animals, but they are extremely important part of our lives and completely dependent on us for their care. The monetary endowment that goes with them is limited to whatever happens to be left in our checking account, but it should feed them for a month or two.

Considering your animals as you plan for the future is a compassionate way to make sure they don't end up in a shelter cage. Older animals aren't easily adopted from shelters, especially if they are grieving for a lost owner. Many childless couples have a deep love for their pets and a strong emotional connection with them.

A last will and testament does not have to be complicated. Forms are available on line from web sites like <www.legalforms.com>. Simply download the form that is appropriate for your state. There is even a form specifically for those who have no children. A free PDF example is offered on most sites, so you can ensure you are purchasing the correct form for your needs. For foundations, trusts, and scholarships use a financial consultant, attorney, or your bank's trust department.

Beyond your spouse and any special considerations, your will is used to dispose of all of your worldly possessions. It doesn't matter if you have a large estate or just a few treasures—having a will gives you control posthumously.

Some families celebrate the tradition of giving precious heirlooms to recipients while the owner is still in good health. These customs give you full control over who receives treasures like your great-grandmother's china, a special pocket watch, or the family Bible.

To make these items more special to those you choose to give them to, use the items during family gatherings and share stories about how they were accumulated. Adding personal connections to the items creates a feeling of heritage for younger generations.

Funeral Planning

Caring for my mother-in-law as she battled cancer educated me in the things that should be done in preparation for our own death. She always said she didn't care what we did after she was gone. She said she wanted the cheapest funeral possible and didn't want anyone to be sad. While we could have given her the first of her requests, I thought she should know what the cheapest funeral would be like for her family. On a day that she felt like getting out of the house, we went to the funeral home to look at the options.

She was shocked to realize the cost of the cheapest funeral and what that did not include. I was relieved as she sat down with the funeral director and expressed her wishes clearly. When she passed away, we were not able to comply with her request not to be sad, but in our sadness we were grateful that she had been involved in her final arrangements. She even chose the flowers she wanted on her casket. There was little for her children to deal with besides their own grief, which was quite enough.

The thought of someone having to make those arrangements was disturbing to John and me. I was unexpectedly emotional at the thought of leaving this earth unknown and unremembered. Logically a pine box or even cremation would not change my eternity. My spirit would not reside in an earthly grave. Regardless of what happens during my funeral or where I am laid to rest, my spirit will be with the Lord.

Paul wrote in 2 Corinthians 5:8, "We are of good courage, I say, and prefer rather to be absent from the body and to be at home with the Lord."

Funerals are for the living, not the dead. By pre-planning we can save our loved ones unnecessary grief and turmoil as they receive the news of our passing. Contacting a funeral director at your local mortuary will get you started.

John and I weren't sure we even wanted funeral services when we are gone. We wondered if it was frivolous to buy a headstone or cemetery plot when there would be no one to visit the graves. When we made up our minds to look into arrangements, we went together. We had no idea there was such a variety of concrete vaults to choose from or that the laws in each state vary as to their uses. The variety of caskets with features and options seemed overwhelming, but the adventure through "mortuary 101" was somewhat fascinating.

Allow yourself a couple of hours minimum for the appointment to plan your final farewell. Being presented with choices of everything from a satin pillow for your head to stationery and the flowers around the casket is daunting. Even as a shopaholic I couldn't wait to leave. However, I'm glad we did it. One phone call to the funeral home when the time comes will take care of everything, and none of our family or friends will carry that burden.

> The righteous man will flourish like the palm tree, He will grow like a cedar in Lebanon. Planted in the house of the LORD, They will flourish in the courts of our God. They will still yield fruit in old age; They shall be full of sap and very green, To declare that the LORD is upright; He is my rock, and there is no unrighteousness in Him *(Psalm 92:12-15)*.

As you age, you will have opportunities to share your wisdom, strength, and grace with the world. God's plan for your life continues as long as there is breath in your body. You will bear fruit into old age as long as you are allowing the Lord to work in you and through you.

No matter where life takes you or what plans you make to meet your emotional, financial, and medical needs, keep the Lord first in your life. His grace is sufficient, and His mercy is new every morning.

Dear Lord Jesus, thank you for the provision you place in my life. Your wisdom is infinite, and your plan is endless. Help us follow your leading into future. We praise you for giving us hope in darkness and direction in confusion. Continue to lead and guide us in your will. In Jesus' name. Amen.

11 GIVING AND RECEIVING ADVICE

He who restrains his words has knowledge, And he who has a cool spirit is a man of understanding.

—Proverbs 17:27

A few years into our struggle with infertility, we stepped away from ministry with children. It was too painful for me. When cancer determined our permanent inability to bear children, we found social events with our friends more difficult than ever.

It was easier to befriend those who remained childless by choice because they never questioned our fertility, and they didn't think we were wrong in not pursuing adoption. However, they didn't understand our pain; they spent hundreds of dollars each year to *prevent* pregnancy. To them, our inability to conceive seemed like a blessing in disguise. Eventually, our social life became limited to a few select friends and each other.

Even after we reached the point of contentment as a childless couple, we donned the moniker assigned to us by infertility as if it were a nametag. We were *childless, infertile, broken.*

We answered questions about children every day. "We don't have any children; God has a different plan for our family." We knew it, we believed it, but our faith didn't stop the stares and questions from the fertile world. *We are an infertile couple. We will never have a normal family.* We watched, powerless to prevent the stigma that attached itself to our marriage. The stigma of childlessness became a spiritual stronghold.

One of the hardest parts of the struggle with infertility is the reaction of friends, family, the church family, and even strangers. For many childless couples there are many events that are almost unbearable. Things that seem so normal in other peoples' lives open wounds and renew the struggles of infertility.

It seemed as if we didn't fit anywhere, especially after we decided to follow God instead of wrestle with Him for control of our purpose. We were older than the young married group in our church but too young for the Silver Slippers. Without children, Mom's Time and Children's Corner were out of the question.

When we were categorized as a couple trying to conceive, we had the prayer support of our church family. In just a few years, we went from extremely active in our church to completely detached from the people we loved and who loved us.

People who did not know us well became instant family and fertility counselors. They had advice on everything from the best sexual practices for conception to all the things that must be wrong in our lives if God was withholding children. Well-meaning strangers offered suggestions of adoption and foster care as if they were revolutionary concepts we had never heard of. The unnecessary advice was acid poured onto our hearts.

The people we loved felt as if they had to walk on eggshells around us. Those who knew us well were aware of our struggle and pain. They wanted to protect us from more hurt, and as a result, pushed us farther away from relationships.

For a while we enjoyed time with friends who had several children. They invited us over to enjoy family dinners, and we enjoyed the laughter and conversation that come only around a table full of multiple generations. They never judged our infertility and never spoke about adoption. It was the bright spot in my week to be with them on leisurely Sunday afternoons.

During one of those wonderful afternoons, I realized the separation between those who are able to have children easily and those who cannot. Dinner was winding down, and the kids were winding up. After separating two of her four children for fighting, she looked at me in her frustration and said," I'm so glad you guys don't have kids, so we only have ours to deal with when we get together." My friend's words hit me like ice water.

We were in the midst of the hardest struggle of our lives, and she was glad we didn't have kids. I would have given anything to have a rowdy four-year-old pulling on his sister's doll or a two-year-old screaming for my attention.

I am sure she saw the tears that threatened to burst from my eyes. But her insensitive words continued. "You don't realize how blessed you are to have some peace and quiet. Just look at it as your silver lining."

John has always been more diplomatic than I have, but even he was ready to let his feelings show. Instead, he just stood up and thanked them for a great afternoon, and we left.

We weren't invited to their home after that. It was as if we had done something offensive in not being happy for our peace and quiet. When I tried to talk to her about it, she told me that I had no idea what it was like to deal with four preschoolers day after day. She was right—I had no idea.

It always surprised me when someone said something so thoughtless. Equally disheartening to me were friends who responded to our desire for children with "You can have one of mine—I promise you won't want them after that." It only made my confusion greater when people could be so glib about the children God had given them.

It also surprised me when they avoided saying anything at all. Being left out of baby news may seem compassionate on the surface, but in reality it adds to the segregation that the childless couple already feels. While it was difficult to hear that people all around us were expecting, it was more painful to realize our friends and family were afraid to tell us. It was as if we had some terrible emotional instability and their news would send us into terminal depression.

When my mom and my brother were afraid to tell me that his wife was expecting their first child, it broke my heart. I wanted to be happy for them and celebrate their family. When they finally decided I had to know before she started showing too much, the news was delivered as if something horrible had happened. "There's something we need to tell you, but we don't want you to get upset," my mom said.

I was expecting her next words to be that she had a terminal illness or that my childhood friend had been in an accident. "Rob and

Kelli are going to have a baby." She said it flatly, trying to hide her joy at becoming a grandmother. At that moment I was happy that I lived half way across the country from them. Not because I wouldn't see Kelli's growing pregnant belly, but because they could enjoy the process without having to worry about me.

I was happy for them! I was about to have a niece or nephew to love, and while that did not take away my desire to be a mother, it was certainly worth celebrating. Not being included in the celebration failed to ease the personal pain I felt because I had no children; it only left me feeling separated from my family even more. It was as if my infertility were an excuse to push me out of their lives. Of course, that was never their intent, but that was how it felt.

My friend Brenda understood my fears. She shared her heart and the struggles she has had in her relationships with her parents and sister since grandchildren entered their family.

We had mixed emotions when my sister became pregnant during an extremely messy divorce. No reconciliation came to the marriage. Her husband, who originally left her to pursue another woman, wanted nothing to do with her or the baby. She elected to raise her baby on her own. Six months after the divorce was final, she gave birth to a beautiful baby girl named Julianne. The loving nature of the baby and her sweet laughter ushered immense joy into all of our lives. I thought she was the most beautiful creature I had ever seen. I took every chance I could to be with her and my family, and Mom and I took turns watching her when my sister was working.

We delighted in every aspect of Julianne's care, from playing with her dolls to watching her splash in the baby pool. She touched a deep part of me. I adored my only little niece, and she captured my heart simply by smiling at me

One day, on one of the rare visits my family made to my home after Julianne was born, we all set out for a walk through my neighborhood. While my husband and I walked with the dogs and chatted with Dad, my mom and sister pushed the baby carriage and stayed behind, deep in conversation. When I slowed my pace to wait for them, their conversation stopped. "Oh, you don't want to be bored by all of our kid talk," my sister said. "We'll catch up with you on the pier."

Feeling rejected, I rejoined the men and kept walking toward the beach. My husband found it odd that they spoke on the phone every day and saw each other several times a week but made no effort to include me in their conversation.

That day was the beginning of many such experiences. As my sister leaned more on the assistance of our mother for child care and financial help, I was pushed farther away from my family. I tried to talk to them about it, but conversations ended painfully. Accusations of jealousy broke my heart. The relationship I shared with my mother and my sister was severed, and I didn't know what to do. I felt broken and alone, not because I couldn't have children, but because my infertility was ripping my mother out of my life.

Our infertility and childlessness has a greater impact on our extended family than we can imagine. They love us and want to protect us. Unfortunately, their protection often translates into rejection.

I did not realize how much I had shared with my mom about the pain of other people's pregnancies. Loving me, she worried about my feelings of distress when I received a shower invitation or footprint-filled announcements. As confusing as the emotional condition caused by infertility is for us, it is even more unclear for those who love us. At least we know when our own mind has changed.

Communication is the key to any successful relationship. We must be careful to mean what we say and say what we mean, without drowning in the emotional swamp.

My friend Siobhan experienced the kid-glove treatment when she desperately wanted a second child. She and her husband knew that Garrett was a miracle, but that didn't stop their longing for a larger family.

Even if you already have a child, you still go through a period of mourning that few people understand. Watching your friends get pregnant with their second, third, and fourth children is painful, but after a while it just doesn't register anymore since many of those same friends don't know how to relate to you. In fact, a friend of mine called me up to tell me she was pregnant again and explained that she wanted to let me know herself because she wanted to make sure I was okay with it. Okay with it? How could I not be? I would never wish infertility on anyone. I would not want another person to feel what this feels like.

Before you find yourself in an uncomfortable confrontation, be clear about what you want. We can master our emotional response if we are prepared.

- Make a list of acceptable reactions to baby news.
- Rejoice with those who rejoice.
- Be honest when you reach the point at which you cannot continue talking about children.
- Treat parenting couples with the same love and respect you desire.
- Leave gracefully when you need to; save hysterics for the privacy of your home or car, or avoid situations that you know are likely to produce those feelings.

If you keep a cool head in the face of baby news, you won't be kept on outer edges, labeled as the childless ones who must be handled gently.

Advice Not Given Is Most Welcome

Most people don't mean any harm with their remarks or reactions. They really are trying to help. It is important for friends and family to keep in mind that a calm exterior may be hiding inward pain, and anguish could be consuming the thoughts of the childless couple.

All of us who have experienced infertility have heard many pieces of advice throughout this journey. "You could always adopt," heard for the millionth time, is not going to change the circumstances that only the childless family can know.

Scripture references to bridling the tongue generally refer to anger, speaking maliciously, lying, or bitter words. James 1:19 says, "This you know, my beloved brethren. But everyone must be quick to hear, slow to speak and slow to anger."

More damage is done to the emotions by the thoughtless words of someone who was quick to speak rather than quick to listen than most people imagine. However, encouragement and even healing can be brought with the silent smile of an understanding friend.

Asking questions of the childless person is less painful. Caring questions are asked initially, but when infertility is revealed, the advice begins. Typical conversations with new friends can be quoted in unison.

"How many children do you have?"

"We don't have any children."

"Oh? How long have you been married?"

"Fifteen years."

"Really? Why don't you have children?"

"We couldn't have them."

"Oh. Well, you can always adopt."

At that point the conversation is over. I have countered by saying, "Really? Wow, I never thought of that." But that is not a good response either. It might make me feel a little better for a minute, but then the offense is tossed to the other person instead of being put to rest. Most often I simply say that we are content with God's design for our childless life.

Not all childless men and women have reached the point of contentment. Unsolicited advice brings their pain to the surface, scraping off the scabs that bring healing and taking them backward emotionally.

The childless couple has a tremendous need for sensitivity from their friends, families, and ministry workers. It is impossible for people with children or people who are childless by choice to know the pain of the infertile couple who has tried everything and come to the end of possibilities.

In some cases, saying nothing is the best answer. If the first thing that comes to mind is advice, stop. Silence is better unless your childless friend asks for your input.

Support is well received when it's framed in love. Expressing your sorrow or understanding is most helpful. Avoid trying to give hope with stories about your sister's son's teacher who got pregnant three weeks after she adopted a baby from China and now has three toddlers and one on the way. Childless couples can appreciate the joy in those stories, but the fact is that it does not work out that way for everyone.

Depending on where a couple is in the journey with infertility, statements from onlookers can be taken differently. Reactions are based on their present situation and may change from time to time. Remember that part of the process that leads to contentment in a home without children is grief. You would never say to a parent who just lost his or her child, "Oh, well—you can always have more." Common sense tells us that would be one of the most hurtful things to say. Yet statements made to the childless couple grieving a miscarriage, a failed adoption, or simply grieving their dreams to become parents are met with insensitive statements, and the implication is that they just need to get over it.

Getting over it is not an option. Women who are not able to have biological children are affected by their plight for a lifetime. Men who have not fathered a child don't forget their infertility. It is constant in their lives, and every time they see a pregnant woman, a tender moment between a parent and child, or a tribute to parenthood on Mother's Day and Father's Day, they are reminded of their barren condition.

That is not to say that they cannot find healing for the pain and live happily, allowing God to lead them through their lives. Nevertheless, thoughtless remarks hurt.

The most hurtful words I experienced when we were struggling with infertility came from an aunt who had no real knowledge of our situation. She had hardly met me, yet felt the need to tell our neighbor that I was like a prostitute. She thought since we had been married a few years and didn't have children that I must be unwilling to have children. Therefore, in her mind, our marital bed was as defiled as a brothel. When I confronted her, she truly had no idea how hurtful she had been. She did not know that we couldn't get pregnant.

In addition to hurtful comments from family and friends, church is often the most difficult emotional event for a childless couple. Dedication Sundays and children's baptism services are difficult to watch for those who won't know what it's like to stand proudly to give their children to the Lord. Mother's Day, Father's Day, and promotions are also hard. Some couples avoid those days altogether.

One of the hardest Sundays of my life came one year on Mother's Day. I hadn't given much thought to the significance of the day until the mothers in the church were asked to stand for an appreciatory round of applause. After the mothers sat down, the church leader at the podium said, "Every woman is a mother to someone; we appreciate you ladies." His words should have rolled off my back, but they made me indignant. Not everyone woman is a mother, and that's okay. We are not defective if we are not mothers. God uses us, and we can celebrate who we are in Christ with or without children as our crown.

Friendships with other women don't come as naturally to childless women as they do for parenting mothers. Women form friendships with other women based on their children's ages. Even friends from high school and college grow distant when they start their families. They spend more time with other women who have children. They have common issues to discuss, advice to share, and stories to laugh about. It is commonality that brings friendships closer. After the weather and current events have been covered, the conversation drops. Sometimes, even small talk is strained, because the perspective of people who have children is different than the perspective of people without children.

I don't think much about the weather—it is what it is, and other than needing to dress accordingly, it doesn't bother me. Mothers take it much more seriously. They have to make sure their children are safe if there is a thunderstorm. Mothers have to adjust their schedules for snow days and, depending on the ages of their children, a trip to the park or the beach requires a bag full of supplies like sunscreen, moist wipes, extra clothes, snacks, and equipment for activities.

Infertility Etiquette

If you and I do not educate people about what they should or should not say to the childless community, they will not know. Don't become so wrapped in the grief that has come with your childlessness that you don't let people know your needs. Most people really do want to understand and to help. They are well-intentioned, but it may be up to you to let them know how things they say affect you.

Here is a guide to share with family, friends, and ministry leaders.

What to Say
- "I'm so sorry for what you're going through."

- "What can I do to help you?"
- "Teach me about what you are going through so I can understand better."
- "It's okay if you need to cry."
- "I'll be praying."
- "In what way can I pray for you?"
- "I'm here if you need me."

You can also say nothing at all—a hug and an understanding smile say a lot.

What Not to Say

- "When are you going to have children?"
- "Have you tried . . .?"
- "Oh, well—just adopt."
- "Are you sure you want to try for a child?"
- "Quit trying so hard. My aunt couldn't get pregnant, but when she finally gave up, she had twins."
- "It's not the end of the world if you don't have kids."
- "There's more to this life than just being a mom."
- "At least you're an aunt. That's fun."
- Also, don't complain about your own children, hinting that childlessness is preferable.

The gift of a friend who will laugh with you and cry with you—without judgment or expectation—is invaluable. Lynn Fries is grateful for the people in her life who have been there with her and her husband through their journey.

> I remember the first time I shared the deep pain I felt because I didn't have children. It was a precious moment to me. I chose to share with someone I trusted and I knew loved me. She and I had shared many deep conversations on many topics. It was easy to tell her what was in my heart. When I started talking, I was very matter of fact—as if I was telling someone else's story. I was used to putting a mask over the pain and walling it in, but as I continued to share with her, the tears began to flow. I glanced at her and saw tears streaming down her face too.
>
> She wept with me. She understood what it meant to me to have kids. We had been teachers together, and she knew my deep love for children. Being able to share this deep disappointment with

someone who loved and cared about me helped my burden be a little lighter. I have been blessed to have several people who took the time to care and show their concern along the way.

I've been ministered to by small and big gestures throughout this journey. A well-timed word or gesture can make a huge difference to a hurting person. There are things that people did to support us and love us that will forever stand out in our memories and hearts. Dear friends gave us money to start a fund in case we decided to adopt, no strings attached. Another friend gave me a Mother's Day card and wrote in it that she was acknowledging how I mothered so many of my students. What a great gift to hear from someone you love that what you do matters!

When I was struggling with fibroid tumors that robbed me of my ability to have kids, I had a hard time tying my shoes. I shared with my brother how much it hurt me to have a tummy like a pregnant woman's when I couldn't even tie my shoes. The next time we were out in public, he noticed my shoe was untied and quietly tied it. I don't have the words to explain what that meant to me. The love and empathy in that gesture, and the look on his face as he did it, will always be in my memory.

When I had surgery for the first time, that same brother brought us our wonderful dog. He knew we needed to love and be loved. It doesn't really matter how small or big the gesture is—the thought and love behind it are what comforts the hurting.

When I had a hysterectomy, one of my sisters-in-law took the time to write to us that she was sorry we had to go through it and that she felt bad that we were losing this dream.

I have a cousin who is always willing to listen to my pain when I need it. She never seems impatient or tells me it's time for me to get over it and move on. I can feel her genuine love for me and that she wants to help me carry my hurt.

Let your friends, family, church family, and ministry leaders know what they can do to show their love and support.

When people are going through things that are hard or not in our experience, we tend to be uncomfortable or avoid it. That is when we need to give our love and support the most.

If someone who is childless brings up his or her pain, the best thing you can do for the person is to validate what he or she is saying. Taking the time to listen, grab his or her hand, and respond with empathy can make all the difference. Putting yourself in the person's place can be helpful, too. What would you need if you were in this situation? What would be comforting to you?

Some of the people who have ministered to me the most have children. They aren't in my situation, but they know and care about me. They take the time to tune into what my world is like. They take the added step of making me feel that my world matters as much as theirs. This might sound like a small thing, but it is big to a person grieving being childless.

They also have the ability not to treat me with kid gloves or act as if I don't want to hear about family lives. They talk freely about themselves and expect me to as well. There is no separation because we have different lives.

If you have a friend or family member who doesn't have children but wanted them, the best thing you can do is to care and find tangible ways to show it. Give them opportunities to talk about the pain if they want to (some won't want to, but don't assume that to be the case), and allow them to be the authorities on how that feels. They are the ones walking down the road. They know what it feels like. Don't try to minimize the hurt or encourage them to move on. Do allow them to express themselves and try to put yourself in their place.

If they lost a child, allowing them to talk freely about anniversaries or how much they miss their child brings healing. Learning about their life and treating it with respect and value also brings a sense of their life counting, too.

If your children are the center of your world, imagine what it would be like not to have this great gift and have to live among many who do have it. When you think about all the ways kids enrich and bless their families, you can truly start to understand how painful this can be to do without. Ask the Lord to show you ways to care, to love and build up your friend. He will be faithful to show you how to help him or her carry or lighten the burden.

Being childless can be a lonely road. Having friends and family who tune in and show in tangible ways how much they care is a tremendous gift.

"Be kind to one another, tender-hearted, forgiving each other, just as God in Christ also has forgiven you" (Ephesians 4:32).

The bottom line is this: in general, people want to be supportive, but sometimes they don't know the best way to do that. Surround yourself with people who have found ways—or are willing to learn—to give you the support and understanding that will help you as you seek to make peace with your childlessness.

Dear Lord, thank you for the friends and family you have given us. Lord, we ask you to forgive us for any hurtful thing we may have said. Put sweet and encouraging words in our mouths and your wisdom as a filter on our tongues. Help us to encourage one another as we walk this world. Let us love one another as you love us. In Jesus' name we pray. Amen.

NOTES

Chapter 1
1. 2002 National Survey of Family Growth.
2. <http://www.lesstoxicguide.ca/print.asp?mode=whole>.
3. <http://pregnancy.lovetoknow.com/wiki/statistics_on_ infertile_couples>. This page is no longer available.

Chapter 2
1. <www.womenshealth.gov>.
2. <http://www.ivfnj.com/html/pcos.html>.
3. <http://www.stanford.edu/class/siw198q/websites/ reprotech/new%20ways %20of%20making%20babies/causefem> This page is no longer available.

Chapter 3
1. <http://www.cdc.gov/nchs/data/databriefs/db12.htl>. This page is no longer available.

Chapter 5
1. <http://www.goacom.com/goatoday/2001/oct/perspective.html> This page is no longer available.
2. The personality definitions here are based on the teaching of Fred, Florence, and Marita Littauer.

Chapter 9
1. Adapted from *One Million Arrows: Raising Your Children to Change the World,* Winepress, 2009. Used with permission.

Chapter 10
1. <http://en.wikipedia.org/wiki/long_term_care_insurance# cite_note-0#cite _note-0>.
2. Continental Association of Funeral and Memorial Societies, 6900 Lost Lake Rd., Egg Harbor, WI 54209. 800-458-5563.